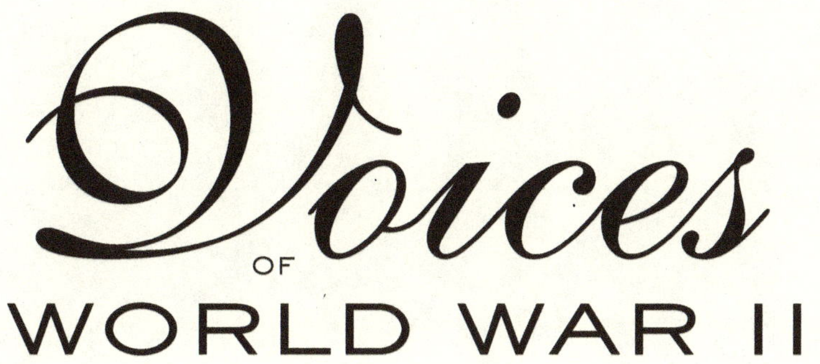

GENE QUIGLEY

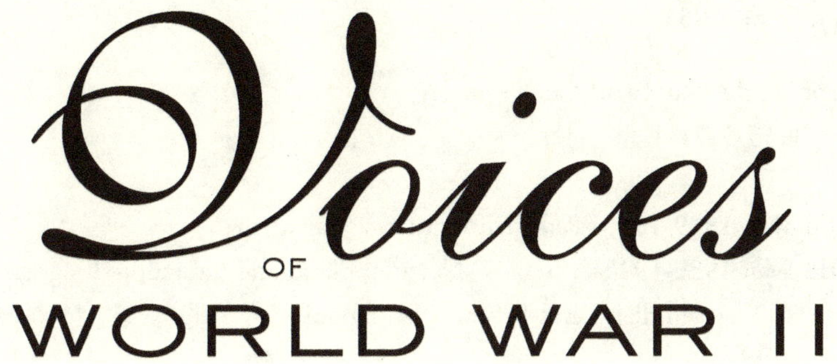

GENE QUIGLEY

Jesperson Publishing

JESPERSON PUBLISHING

100 Water Street • P.O. Box 2188
St. John's • NL • Canada • A1C 6E6
www.jespersonpublishing.ca

Library and Archives Canada Cataloguing in Publication

Quigley, Gene, 1964-

Voices of World War Two / Gene Quigley.
ISBN 1-894377-21-4

1. World War, 1939-1945--Personal narratives, Canadian.
2. World War, 1939-1945--Veterans--Newfoundland and Labrador--Biography.
3. Soldiers--Newfoundland and Labrador--Biography. I. Title.

D768.154.N49Q84 2006 940.54'81718 C2006-903979-8

Editor: Annamarie Beckel

All photographs, except where noted, were provided by the men and women who were interviewed.

Front cover photographs:
Top, from left: Art White, Len Williams, Gordon Drodge, Austin Smith, Taylor French, Angus Legrow, Hubert Thistle, and Bruce Taylor.
Bottom, from left: Eric Thomson Baggs, Jessie Windsor [Goodyear], and Thomas Joseph Houlihan

We acknowledge the financial support of The Canada Council for the Arts for our publishing activities.

We acknowledge the support of the Department of Tourism, Culture and Recreation for our publishing activities.

Printed in Canada

CONTENTS

ACKNOWLEDGEMENTS

This book could not have been written without the cooperation of the men and women who patiently responded to my interviews, and I am grateful for their help, as well as for the photographs they generously provided for use in this volume. I would like to thank the late Austin Smith, who was one of the first veterans I interviewed. He was in failing health but still had time for my ceaseless inquiries regarding his campaign in Italy.

And lastly I must thank my wife Cindy for her patience and encouragement – not to mention one or two good ideas.

INTRODUCTION

The foundations for this book were in progress long before I knew it. As a young boy growing up in St. John's, I was fascinated by anything related to the Second World War, even though the war had ended almost 20 years before I was born. I went from playing with toy soldiers to reading comics about the war.

I read books about World War II and watched movies and documentaries. I found the documentaries the best, and I can still sit down and be captivated by them. Next I began cutting war-related articles out of newspapers. In 1997, I started a family history, which included relatives who had served in the war.

Most of what I read or saw about the war is from an American or British point of view, and one purpose of this project was to find out how Newfoundlanders contributed to the war effort. Most of us know someone who was in the Royal Navy or Royal Artillery, but beyond that, people know very little of what Newfoundlanders did and how important their contributions were.

For many Newfoundlanders, World War II was the defining event of their lives and their generation. Men and women volunteered for all branches of the Canadian, British, and American armed forces. Some volunteered with a sense of duty, some with a sense of adventure, many with both. There were those who even lied about their age to get into the armed forces. All acknowledge the brutality and ugliness of war, but few regret their decision to serve.

More than 60 years have passed since the end of the war, and veterans are passing away at an alarming rate. These people are walking encyclopedias, and although Herb Wells in *Under the White Ensign* and *Comrades In Arms* and Col. G.W.L. Nicholson in *More Fighting Newfoundlanders* have done some excellent work, very little has been done to preserve the veterans' oral histories. Over the past three years I have conducted more than 60 interviews with 32 veterans. My first interview was with the late Austin Smith of Mount Pearl in February 2003. His interview just blew me away. Before the interview, I had thought that I had a little knowledge of the war, but most of the things he spoke about I had never heard before. He was a tank commander in Italy with the Canadian Army and had been involved in a lot of heavy fighting. I had a number of interviews with Mr. Smith, and I went to the library before each one so I could keep up with what he was telling me. Through him, I met a number of his friends who were also in the Canadian Army, and that is how I gathered people to interview. Of each person I went to see, I would always ask who else I should interview, which always led to more names and phone numbers.

I've included a cross-section of people who served in the various armed forces. I regret, however, that I had the opportunity to interview only one man from the Royal Newfoundland Regiment and no one from the Royal Canadian Naval Volunteer Reserve, and I apologize to those veterans that I do not have chapters for those branches.

Because so much time has passed since the end of World War II, the possibility for errors does exist. To help ensure accuracy, the veterans who were interviewed proofread their individual narratives, but any errors are mine, and I apologize for all errors and omissions.

The majority of stories in the following pages come from Newfoundlanders or from people who have a strong Newfoundland connection, and the purpose of this book is not only to find out how Newfoundlanders contributed to the war effort, but also to keep the memories and experiences of our veterans alive. These personal histories, in the veterans' own words, speak for themselves and bring history to life.

CHAPTER 1

CANADIAN ARMY

When Great Britain declared war on Germany on September 3, 1939, Newfoundland, being a colony of Britain, was at war too, but Newfoundland did not have a military of its own. With the defeat of France in 1940, Canada saw Newfoundland's lack of a military as a threat to its safety, and Canada was forced into a closer defence relationship with Newfoundland. In June 1940 elements of the Canadian Army arrived in Newfoundland, and Newfoundlanders joined up.

In the fall of 1941, these eight young men, all close friends, went to Lester's Field in St. John's to join the Sherbrooke Fusiliers, which was an infantry regiment of the Canadian Army. In addition to those named in the photograph, there were George Gulliver, Kevin Griffiths, and Pat Lewis. In this chapter are some of their stories.

The Sherbrooke Fusiliers served in Newfoundland from August 15, 1941, to February 19, 1942.

Left to Right: Art White, Len Williams, Gordon Drodge, Austin Smith, Taylor French, Angus Legrow, Hubert Thistle, Bruce Taylor.

AUGUSTINE AUSTIN SMITH

DATE ENTERED SERVICE:
October 1941

CAMPAIGNS:
Sicily, Italy, Northwest Europe

DECORATIONS:
Service Star 1939-1945, Italian Star, France and Germany Star, Defence of Britain, Canadian Volunteer Service Medal with clasp, Dutch Medal of Remembrance, Victory Medal, Canadian Legion Medal 75 years

REGIMENT:
Sherbrooke Fusiliers 2nd Division, Three Rivers 1st Division

SERIAL #: D47063

I was born on October 9, 1923, in St. Jacques, Fortune Bay, Newfoundland, to Martin and Elizabeth Smith. In 1932, during the Depression, we moved from St. John's to Mount Pearl. Park Avenue was just a little mud track then.

With the outbreak of the Second World War, I, like many people, was interested in joining the armed forces. I attempted to get in the British forces, but I was turned down for all three branches because I was only 17 years old. I decided to try the Canadian armed forces. This time I lied about my age and they accepted me. For me it was more or less an adventure, and in addition to that, all my friends were joining up.

Eventually, we left Newfoundland and went to Debert, Nova Scotia. It was here that we transformed from an infantry regiment to a tank regiment. After a period of training here, the regiment went overseas. Our first stop was Aldershot, England. We were here training for quite a long time before even seeing a tank. Once we received the tanks we started to shift around quite a bit.

Next we went to Denoon, Scotland, where we learned to waterproof the tanks. We used to go out in an LST, a landing ship tank, and come in on the beach and land, preparing for the second front.

In the meantime we were the 2nd Division, and the 1st Division was going to Sicily in July 1943. They were looking for volunteers for a three-month stint to get some battle experience. Once you came back, you could be an instructor. I decided to go.

A little more than five weeks later the campaign in Sicily was over. Then [General] Montgomery came and gathered us all around, congratulated us and everything else as a fine bunch of fighting men. But I will always remember the last part of his speech: "Just remember, the only good German is a dead one." That is how he closed it off. I guess at the time and place he was probably right, but there were still a lot of good German people.

When we got to Italy, we suffered so many casualties in different places we did not get back to our regiment. There were cases in Italy where they turned around and had to use cooks and clerical staff, put a rifle in their hands, and put them up on the front lines. That's how short it was. They kept us down there and this is why I stayed with the Three Rivers Regiment.

In Italy we fought against the Hermann Goering Division and it got so bad at the Moro River just before Ortona we had to call a three-day truce to clean up the wounded and the dead. I remember speaking to one sergeant in that German division who was with the Red Cross. He came beside the tank, spoke good English and asked for a cigarette. He said, "You know, this is ridiculous, this is awful. Look at all the bodies." We could not manoeuvre the tank without driving on top of one. I don't think there was one German less than six feet tall in the Hermann Goering Division. They were regular soldiers. They were with our Red Cross, cleaning up, as he said, "Here we are picking up each other's dead and wounded and tomorrow or the next day we will be blowing each other's brains out." He was good to talk to and everything else.

On the other side of it you had the SS and they were fanatics. They had no regard for life or anything else. They would put up their hands and surrender and there would be some guy hid in the back somewhere with a couple of potato mashers [grenades], and if you advanced to take a prisoner they would let it drive at you.

In my opinion, any man who went into action and said he wasn't scared was lying to himself and everyone around him. I have been into combat where you're the one who is going into the action. He is the one who is just sitting there waiting until he sees the whites of your eyes. You don't know when it is going to start. Everything is so still and quiet. I have gotten so sick, I've just thrown up, knotted up in the stomach, and everything else until after the first shot was fired. After that you had to fight to survive. In every action that we went in on, I used to say to myself, "If we are going to get it, we'll get it really fast because it would take something heavy to take us out."

I remember another action in Italy. We went on a patrol to a place called Aquino airport. We went up with six tanks and came back with two, my crew and the crew of the other tank. They had been fired upon and their tank was damaged. I was the only tank to come out in one piece. I suppose the only reason for that was that I was the last in the column, and when they started the action I tried to see some other way around it. I didn't bull right in, as the fella says, you know. And on the way back he [the Germans] opened up, and I don't know what he fired on us, but I felt the tank go down in a hole when the shell hit in front of us. It was the same as someone putting a person in front of a sandblaster, and the flash, by God, yes. The only thing I heard when

I dropped to the floor was the gunner saying, "Smitty is hit." I knew no more until we got back.

When we got back and I came around, I had flash blindness. I could not see. They wanted me to go back. But there was no tanker willing to go back unless he was bloody well seriously wounded. Because what was happening down in Italy, you might have been a tanker, but once you were injured and removed, you would not go back to the tank, you would go to the infantry. No tanker wanted to go to the infantry. What we used to do is take care of one another if your wound could be treated undercover.

Prior to us moving into the Liri Valley there was a huge artillery barrage. The 166th Newfoundland Royal Artillery gave us firepower and support. The night that they opened up the guns down there you could easily sit down and read a paper on the back deck of a tank. We were all there under the rise and the guns below us. You could see the 25-pound shells go right over us. They kept that up just about the whole night. The Rapido River was alongside. They used to have to form bucket brigades to bring up water to pour on the barrels of the guns to cool them off because they were firing on their own.

Another time going up the Liri Valley, a friend that I had met before we got into action, a sergeant whose first name was Huey, I looked and I saw him walking around with his two legs apart. I said, "Where are you going?" "Up front," he says. I was talking to him for a few minutes. He had been wounded a short time before and had just been released from a field hospital. There was a bullet that went through his leg, through the fleshy part, went across, and went through the head of his penis and followed out through. Here he was all swaddled up. He was going in then and he wasn't, what you call, over his wound. Nobody wanted any part of the infantry.

Another aspect of Italy that I remember was the mountains. I mean they had a mountain there and across the valley another mountain. We would be going up the mountain road in our tanks. What he [the Germans] would usually do was put Rachet mines in. One tank would run over it and drive it down a bit. Probably six or seven tanks would go over it before the last tank would explode it. The road was probably just the width of a tank. You could not turn around and get back, and you could not go over the side because there was probably a couple of thousand feet drop. The Germans would be on the other side with a few 88's [anti-tank, anti-aircraft gun]. And he would have this front tank, and a Tellermine up here and knock that one out. As a result, he might have six or eight tanks in between and go BANG, BANG, BANG. These 88's, they were powerful guns that had a really long barrel. I mean they could knock down aircraft at 40,000 feet out of the sky.

Of all the fighting forces that we supported, the best ones to my mind were the Gurkhas [members of principal Hindu community in Nepal known for their military prowess]. I don't think there was one more than five feet tall or close to five feet. An English officer would take them in and their own officer would take them out. They would not come out for an English officer. They had a knife, a Gurkha knife, and how sharp it was, and believe me, it was sharp. I remember the Gurkhas were in a patrol just across from Ortona. They came across this German machine gun nest and all three were asleep on the gun. What they did, they slit the throats of the two on the outside and left the guy in the middle. They also took the barrel of the gun. You can imagine what he felt like when he woke up. We heard that an order came out after that, the Germans were taking no more Gurkha prisoners, shoot on sight.

After difficult fighting in Ortona, in May and June, we went through the Liri Valley, into the Hitler Line, and then the Gustav Line. We were in the fifth battle of Cassino and all hell broke loose there. I lost quite a few buddies in that one. I mean it was a real killing ground there up the Liri Valley.

Eventually we'll say, yes, the Americans will say that they liberated Rome. We were only a few miles outside of Rome, but on account of protocol or whatever the hell it was, we could not go into Rome. It was the same when we took Florence. My crew and I were in Florence five days before they even declared it an open city. The Americans did the same thing in Palerno, Sicily.

We fought our way up through Italy, through Lake Trasimene, up through the Gothic Line, and through the Plains of Bologna where we winter-lined.

In the spring the second front was going in. When D-Day occurred, they moved us back. Now [Lieutenant-General] Simonds, who was the supreme commander of the Canadian forces, wanted all the Canadian Army together, because at the time, we were fighting with the British Eighth Army. He wanted all the Canadian troops together in France. We left and sailed out of Naples, and went across to southern France and up through Marseilles. We then joined with our Canadian forces, which was after D-Day. This is why Lady Astor referred to us as "the D-Day Dodgers."

By the time we reached France and got reorganized we were well battle experienced. We went through France, Belgium, Holland, and the Scheldt Estuary, and came down through Antwerp. And of course, once we got out of France and started going through Belgium and Holland, a lot of us used to get split up. Sometimes they would take a troop of us and support a company of infantry. We could stay with them until the action was over. Once that was finished, we would be asked to go help someone else. We were always on loan.

Once we arrived in northwestern Europe, we were there until the war was over. I remember Holland well. In Arnhem, we were supporting the Yanks just for firepower, and it was sad to see those poor buggers. They would go out in these canvas boats just outside Nijmegen on the Waal River to go across the river. They were just torn to pieces. This was the US 82nd Airborne, who were a parachute outfit. When they came in, we went in for support. The trouble was that the Germans were dug into the bank, and although we would shell it and they would stop, the minute we would stop firing, they were up again with the machine gun. They had a perfect shelter there, the way the bank was made. One thing that I noticed about the Yanks, when they had an objective, they did not care about the cost.

The Germans had all sorts of obstacles in our way, tank traps, anti-tank guns, mines with booby traps around that, and everything was heavily fortified. If the engineers went in to do anything, they were the ones who got it. They had Pak 75's [anti-tank guns] along with their tanks. They could sit and wait until they saw the whites of your eyes.

I remember one place, I cannot recollect the name of the town, but there was a small bridge, enough to make a tank trap, and there was a small bridge over it. As we came upon it, we started getting anti-tank gunfire from the bridge. We went over the round and finally we got enough shells in on the bridge where the gun was. After it was all over, we went across the bridge. The Germans on the gun were about 10 years old. There were about seven or eight of them. We had killed five or six. It was sad to see, I mean, we were young ourselves but these were only kids.

We went through several places in Holland liberating towns. When we used to go through a town, if the townspeople were out waving, we knew there were no Germans around. But if the streets were bare, all you had to do was look down at the basement windows and see them down there with their fingers making the sign V for victory. We knew the Germans were around somewhere.

Another aspect of Holland was that the people were actually starving. It was near the end of the war. We had to turn around and defy the Germans, go against them at all odds, and open up a corridor to get the food in. What we did was bring the tanks up the line, and the trucks went in with the food supplies. We called a truce, and I must say they honoured it. We stayed until the trucks came back.

When we went into Germany, things were far different from liberating towns in Holland and Belgium. You could see a lot of people were downtrodden from the war, and of course, we were the invaders. While in Germany, we also freed a political prisoner camp called Endchede. There were a couple of hundred prisoners and they were like skeletons. It was not like Buchenwald, but they were treated much the same way.

One thing that I found in the army was the lack of communication. You were not brought in on briefings of any measure. The time frame did not allow your commanding officer, like our troop lieutenant, to come back and sit down and tell us what we were going to do. He would come down and say, "Okay, byes, we're going up in five minutes." So where the hell are we going? He could say the name of the place. But we did not know the ground or what the intelligence reports were. Now in the Liri Valley we knew we were up against the Gothic and Hitler Lines, but what was there we did not know. You had to feel your way out, we'll say.

On the day that the war was over in Europe, we were in a field not quite three miles from Wageningen, Holland, where they signed the armistice to end the war in Europe. We sat down, looked at one another, had a cigarette and made some Compo tea. Then we looked at one another: we are out of a job, what are we going to do?

After the war they wanted me to stay in the army. The sergeant major of Longueuil wanted me to be the quartermaster, but at the time I had enough of spit-and-polish. I was discharged in District 4 of Montreal in October 1946.

I thank God every day that I am still here, but a lot of my buddies did not make it. It was really something, some actions that we were in: we had infantry with us and to see them just get mowed down.

When he passed away on June 22, 2004, Austin Smith had the longest residency of anyone in Mount Pearl, having moved there at the age of nine. □□

LESLIE TAYLOR FRENCH

DATE ENTERED SERVICE:
October 7, 1941

CAMPAIGNS:
D-Day landing, Northwest Europe

DECORATIONS:
Service Star 1939-1945, Defence of Britain, France and Germany Star, Victory Medal, Canadian Voluntary Service Medal with clasp, Canadian Centennial Medal, Canadian 125th Anniversary Medal, Queen's Jubilee 25-year Medal, Canadian Decoration, Queen's Jubilee 50-year Medal, Dutch Medal of Remembrance

REGIMENT: Sherbrooke Fusiliers

SERIAL #: D47059

I was born in Bay Roberts, Newfoundland, on April 28, 1923, to Nathan and Agnes French. At the age of nine my family and I moved to St. John's.

When the war started in September 1939, I was not old enough to join the army. At the age of sixteen, however, I tried the navy, the forestry

[Newfoundland Forestry Unit], and the artillery. At the recruiting office there was a Max Chambers who was in charge. Every time that I would go there to join something, he would tell me to go the hell home out of it. He knew that I was not old enough and that my father, who was in the first war, had passed away. In addition to that, my older brother Wilf was in the 166th [Royal Artillery]. I was home with my mother and money was not plentiful. You needed every dollar to stay alive.

There was no way that I could get in any of the Newfoundland forces because they were so familiar with me. Now my good friend Len Williams was in much the same position as he had three brothers already in the service.

Prior to joining the army, I worked as a mail carrier along with Len for the Department of Posts and Telegraphs. We had heard that some of the lads had already gone to Lester's Field and joined up there. We went there, had our medical and some other tests. When our parents found out, they stopped us. We then decided: If we cannot join the army, we won't go to work. We quit our jobs, but then I became concerned that we would not have a cent to buy a few fags [cigarettes]. After three or four days we persuaded our parents to sign an oath agreeing to let us join. This is how we ended up in the Canadian forces. When we joined the Sherbrookes in 1941, it was an infantry regiment, and we were assigned to C Company.

In February 1942, we left Newfoundland and went to Debert, Nova Scotia. I was stationed there between two and three months when I was sent to England for a wireless instructor course, which lasted about three months. It was a difficult course but I got through it. I was then a qualified instructor, but I did not like that. After the course was over, I waited for the regiment to come over.

The regiment arrived in July or August and the first place that we were stationed was Aldershot. This was strictly a military town. We were there for quite a long time in places like Hedley Downs and Worthing. We continued training with all types of schemes in order to prepare for the invasion. Some of the schemes [mock battles and training exercises] lasted a day while others lasted between two and three weeks. We did this under conditions that we expected to find in France. We learned how to waterproof our tanks in Denoon and practised landing from LCT's. These landing craft used to hold eight Shermans, which meant the LCT carried quite a load because each one weighed 32 tons. By the time the invasion came around we were well trained. As a matter of fact, we were trained to death in England, and everybody was sort of getting pissed off. We had been waiting long enough, and we wanted to put to use what we had learned.

Before we loaded up for the invasion, we went into this holding area that had barbed wire all around it. Once you went in there, you could not get out due to security reasons. We boarded the landing craft in a place called Gosport just outside Southampton. We were on that frigging thing all night, and once you got on it there were no getting off. On the way over, there was water on the landing craft because the front door wasn't closed properly. We waited for daylight, and once dawn came, what a sight. There were ships of every size and type as far as your eyes could see. When you looked overhead, you could see the fighters and bombers. To the ordinary soldier in the rank and file, you did not know what was going on. You had to depend on someone else, you know, okay, move now.

We landed on Juno Beach at a place called Bernieres-sur-Mers. We were part of the 3rd Canadian Infantry Division, 2nd Canadian Armoured Corps. It consisted of three regiments: the Fort Garry Horse, 1st Hussars, and ourselves. Both of these were assault battalions from western regiments. We were in support of the 6th, 7th, and 8th Brigades of the 3rd Division. We were reserve and were supposed to move through once they reached their objective. That was the plan, but it did not work out that way because, first of all, a lot of tanks in the assault force had what they called DD's. They had flotation devices on them, and they would float on their own power. There were a lot of those frigging things that sank before they got ashore. They sank either because something happened to their flotation or they landed in too deep of water. Even though they had waterproofing gear on, you still had an exhaust pipe and an intake. If these were 12 feet high and you landed in water that was 15 feet high, then this is where they stayed. They would have sucked water down in their intake that went into the engine, and that was the end.

For most of us this was our first action. Incidentally there were three of us from Newfoundland in the one tank. I was the gunner, my good buddy, Len Williams, was the driver, and Kev Griffiths was the co-driver. In my tank our objective was Carpiquet, which was an airport just outside Caen. We got to our objective all right, as a matter of fact we got a half dozen tanks right on the airport. But they [the Germans] had the bloody thing ringed with 88's, which are anti-tank, anti-aircraft guns. The 88-mm was one of the most advanced weapons ever invented. If they fired at you, and even if they missed, it could make you wet in your pants. As a result we had to fall back and we consolidated for the day.

The next day we realized that Jerry [the Germans] had gotten into our encampment the night before. I think we lost about 21 tanks, but they did not drive us back. We stayed there and we accounted for more than our losses between tanks, half-tracks, and one thing or the other. This was the biggest battle that we had in the entire war. The enemy was made up of the 21st and 1st Panzer Divisions. Most of these troops had been and still were Hitler Youth. These were the do-or-die people because they were so indoctrinated with the brainwashing and all the bullshit.

We were supposed to have Carpiquet Airfield on the first day, but thirty days later we still did not have it. They dropped thousands of tons of stuff, and the artillery pounded Caen to pieces. We were the first tanks in Caen, and when we arrived there was nothing left. It was just as flat as the floor.

Falaise, that was a son of a bitch of a place. We moved up there in the nighttime with our tanks. I remember they used artificial moonlight by using searchlights to reflect off the clouds. It was just like day. By this time I was a crew commander and I had my own tank. When we got to Falaise, we just moved in, in the dark, waiting for daylight to come. That is a scary situation because you don't know what the hell you are going to find when it turns daylight. When we stopped, I was looking out the turret of the tank. It was just coming on daylight and I saw this barrel in the drain. I hopped out and everything was quiet at this time. Lo and behold, this was a 45-gallon drum full of Calvados. In France they make a drink that is stronger than anything that you can get here. It is called Calvados, which is the name of a province in Normandy. The farmers make apple cider first, and then they distil it. I'm going to tell you, that frigging stuff will knock your head off. We used to carry two jerry cans full of water. We threw the water out and filled them up with Calvados. We did not drink any of it there, but once we got out of Falaise, I rationed out the Calvados and had a party. With armour you can only go for so long before you would have to come out, possibly for 48 hours, for repairs.

Emmerich, which is in the Ruhr Valley, is where the Sherbrooke Fusiliers crossed the Rhine on those floating bridges. We had a bit of a bad experience there, but we did get in Emmerich after we crossed over. There was not a hell of a lot of tanks there because tanks avoid towns if there is any way they can because they are too vulnerable. You have a job to defend yourself when you have infantry there with panzerfausts, which are anti-tank weapons, and snipers in the rubble.

Once we reached Emmerich the place was flat. Most of the streets there were like the way most of Europe is, row housing. As all the houses were connected, the Germans knocked out the basement walls so they could walk the whole length of the street without coming up. This was a factory town, and for the most part, what was left were smokestacks from the factories.

I remember the lieutenant asked me to do a little "recce" or recognisance with him because things were really quiet. The two of us got out, left our tanks. We had four tanks there, the whole troop. Down behind one of the buildings we saw this frigging movement. There was a self-propelled gun down there. Obviously, we had been spotted by the enemy from a smokestack. I mean, we were no sooner out of the tank and the mortar fire started to come in on us. So I said, "Ed, come on. Let's make tracks out of here and get back in that frigging tank." Mortars would have no effect on the tank. It would just hop off as if you were throwing snowballs at it.

There were walkways there made of brick, and we were in these because if you got a direct hit, it had to drop right in the walkway. Most would go over and blow before they got in there. We then took off, and Roger Bannister [the first man to run the mile in less than four minutes] had nothing on us. The byes saw us coming and we put one foot on the tank and the other down in the turret. That was a scary place for tanks and it was a good place to be out of.

Prior to D-Day I did not know what it was like to be afraid. You are more anxious than anything. Now, after your baptism of fire and you see what can happen to you and you know that you have to go in that situation again, then you're afraid. Then you're afraid until the armistice is signed. I mean, anyone who tells you that they are not afraid is crazy. They are not telling you the truth or they are not very noble people.

When the war ended I was in England. I had landed in D-Day and fought right up through Germany, and they sent me back for a battle course. Thinking back, it was only an excuse to give me a break. When you look at an armoured regiment, there are only about 250 personnel that are doing the actual fighting. The rest are in supply or administration. I was one of the ones, you could almost count them on one hand, who was still around. They gave me a break.

After the war I came home and joined the reserve. I was with the 56th Field Squadron, the engineers section, for almost 20 years.

Taylor French currently resides in Mount Pearl. □□

* Picture, page 25
This picture was taken in Scotland in 1942. I was dressed in a Scottish Highland outfit and not a Sherbrooke Fusiliers uniform. My mother was from Scotland, and I felt that I had some Scots blood in me. In addition, my friends and I would go to visit my aunt, who lived in Scotland, when we were training there.

LEONARD MELVIN WILLIAMS

DATE ENTERED SERVICE:
October 7, 1941

CAMPAIGNS:
D-Day landing, Northwest Europe

DECORATIONS:
Service Star 1939-1945, Defence of Britain, France and Germany Star, Victory Medal, Canadian Voluntary Service Medal with clasp

REGIMENT: Sherbrooke Fusiliers

SERIAL #: D47060

Len Williams was born in July 1923, the son of Harold and Susannah Williams. He grew up on Franklyn Avenue in St. John's and attended the Springdale Street school. Prior to joining the army, Williams worked as a mail carrier for the Department of Posts and Telegraphs.

With the outbreak of the Second World War, Williams already had three older brothers in the service. Undoubtedly his desire to join the army met strong opposition from his parents. Eventually they did sign an oath giving their consent for their son to join the Canadian Army. As a result the Williams family had four sons in the service. There was Fred in the Royal Navy, Jack in the 166th Newfoundland Field Regiment, Royal Artillery, Cec in the 59th Newfoundland Heavy Regiment, Royal Artillery, and Len in the Canadian Army.

After a long period of training, Williams saw his first action on D-Day. He came ashore at Juno Beach in an LCT [landing craft tank]. He was driving a Sherman tank as part of C Squadron. There were two other Newfoundlanders in the tank with Williams. They were Taylor French, the gunner, and Kev Griffiths, the co-driver. The following day, D+1, on June 7, 1944, the tank they were in had a mechanical failure. When this occurred they all had to bail out of the tank and they headed for the hedgerows. They then had a little group to decide what they were going to do. Should they stay where they were or make an attempt to get out of there? The three from Newfoundland decided they wanted to get the hell out of there, while the sergeant did not want to go. He did not want to stay by himself either.

They got up and took off across this big open field. The Germans had everything zeroed in on this area, like mortars dropping everywhere. Somehow they all got across and made it back to their own lines. If they had stayed where they were, they could have become prisoners of war because the land that they had won had been retaken by the Germans. The three young men from Newfoundland then went back into action in different tanks.

Williams was injured in action on the Leopold Canal in Belgium. This was the action to free the port of Antwerp, which for the most part was done by Canadians. The Sherbrooke Fusiliers were in support of this action. He was injured when an 88 shell came in through the back of the tank. When a round came through one of these tanks, it would be just the same as throwing a rock through a window; the slivers of steel would go everywhere. All this went through his back and spine and came in on an angle and killed the co-driver. The crew in the turret had already bailed out. Williams somehow crawled out too. He was trying to crawl to a ditch where they were, but he could not make it. They got out, dragged him into the shelter and brought him to the hospital.

On October 8, 1944, Len Williams, at the age of 21, died in the hospital as a result of the injuries he received ten days before on the Leopold Canal. He is buried in a cemetery called Lier in Belgium, which is not far from Brussels. His three brothers, Fred, Jack, and Cec, survived the war. □□

The information about Len Williams comes from an interview with Taylor French, May 12, 2003.

Len Williams, Canadian Army.

KEVIN JOSEPH GRIFFITHS

DATE ENTERED SERVICE:
September 30, 1941

CAMPAIGNS:
D-Day Landing, Northwest Europe

DECORATIONS:
Service Star 1939-1945, Defence Medal, France and Germany Star, Canadian Volunteer Service Medal and clasp, Victory Medal, Dutch Medal

REGIMENT:
Sherbrooke Fusiliers, 1st Canadian Armoured Carrier Regiment (Kangaroos)

SERIAL #: D47057

I was born on July 18, 1923, in St. John's to George and Alice Griffiths. I grew up on Hamilton Avenue and went to school at Holy Cross. I remember the Depression years with my father losing his job and my mother passing away at a young age.

With the war on I tried to join the navy [Royal Navy], but they told me I was colour blind so they would not take me. I tried to get in the air force but there seemed to be a lot of red tape, so I said, "Forget that." I gave up trying for a while. My next choice was the Canadian Army which was located on Lester's Field. We gave them our names and whatnot, and we had to go back for needles and all that type of crap. I will never forget Frenchie [Taylor French] who was ahead of us. I said, "Did that hurt?" "No," he said, "there is nothing to it." And then bang, he hit the floor. I joined the army because I figured it was my duty to go, and a lot of young fellas were joining.

Once we were enlisted, we did very little training here. We used to do route marches into a little store in around Hamilton Avenue called Hayes. This was located where the present-day Bank of Nova Scotia is. While there, we would have a chat, and then return to barracks.

Eventually, we left Newfoundland on some piece of junk that I would not even call a boat. There was a lot of vomit on it. We got off the boat at Halifax and ended up in Debert. We were not there very long before we had a forest fire, and we were fighting fires because the hospital was there too. While there, we changed from an infantry regiment to an armoured one. Any fella who could not speak English was transferred to a French regiment. After Debert, we went over to England aboard the *Queen Elizabeth*. We did more training in Aldershot and we had a lot of schemes or training exercises. I did training in wireless, gunnery, loader operator, and as a co-driver. We also did a lot of training up in Denoon, Scotland, where we learned how to waterproof the tanks.

Early in June 1944 we were preparing to load up for the invasion. We had to line up all the armoured vehicles in the streets, which went back quite a way. Once we boarded, the invasion was held off for a few days due to poor weather, but we had to stay aboard the LST [landing ship tank] anyway.

On June 6, 1944, we are on our way in an LST to somewhere in France. I never really gave it much thought. This was all like training for us. We landed in the water and we got in as far as we could get with the landing craft. Then we ran the Shermans off into the water. The tanks had these big funnels on them for the exhaust. When you got ashore all you had to do was drive in and that fell off. We did not receive much resistance on the way ashore. I thought it was just like a game until I saw these tanks and trucks burning. I knew it was no game anymore.

We were supposed to go into Caen that day but we never got there. Then we got bogged down and that fuckin' tank we had got caught in the mud, and she wouldn't come out of it. She would just skid. They took the major out and sent us a corporal or a sergeant. He said, "Byes, we're going to stay here now." I said, "Look, if you want to stay, stay, but this chicken is going back with the rest of them." As a result we all left and we had to rear echelon. We had no infantry in front of us, well there were, but not in our area. On our way back, there were mortars flying all around. We made it back and when we did, an officer informed us that we should dig a slit trench that night as we might be visited by the Germans. We said, "Fuck that, they're not coming tonight." But they did. They came over in aircraft and bombed us. The next morning we dug holes as far as China. After this we never did get back together.

Another time we were in an orchard and we ran into the SS, and I guarantee they were something else. We had three tanks, and they started to fire at us. We had two machine guns, one in the turret and one with the co-driver. We also had a 75-mm that could fire armour-piercing shells. They used to come out, and instead of giving up, they would just take off to their own lines, and we'd open up our machine guns.

Then we went into Falaise. There were supposed to be five or six lines going down, tanks and infantry, while the artillery was firing tracers. We were following them, and all of a sudden I could not hear a damn sound. I said, "Bye, there is something wrong. We are after losing our way." We started to zigzag back and forth. I opened up the turret to check. Here I saw all these fellas coming with their hands behind their backs. I said, "Hey, buddies, what outfit is this?" They never answered and just kept going. They were Germans. We did not do much in Falaise because we did not know where the hell we were. Finally I got on back of this tank and realized they were A Squadron, which was with us.

By the time Falaise was almost over, I had blood poisoning under my arm, which put me in the hospital for a week or so. I was then finished with the tanks because all they were taking were drivers. When I got out of the hospital, they were taking fellas of any use to the Kangaroo Regiment. They picked us out and told us we had to go. Now some fellas might have been upset at leaving their regiment, but I didn't give a fuck where I was. Our job was to transport troops into action so that they would not be injured on the way to battle. I was with this regiment until the end of the war. When the war was over, I was just waiting to go home.

Kevin Griffiths passed away on March 30, 2006. □□

HUBERT THISTLE

DATE ENTERED SERVICE:
September 1941

CAMPAIGNS:
D-Day landing

DECORATIONS:
Service Star 1939-1945, France and Germany Star, Defence Medal, Canadian Volunteer Service Medal, Victory Medal

REGIMENT: Sherbrooke Fusiliers

SERIAL #: D47054

I was born on March 1, 1924, in St. John's to Alec and Rose Thistle. I grew up on Mayor Avenue and attended Holloway and Parade Street schools. With the outbreak of the Second World War, I attempted to join the Royal Navy, but I was stopped one day before the draft left because of my age, which was 17. Like a lot of young men at the time, I was interested in adventure. Another motivating factor for me was that my father had been in the First World War with the Newfoundland Regiment and had fought at Beaumont Hamel. As a result, when the Sherbrooke Fusiliers of the Canadian Army came to town, a bunch of us joined them. While in St. John's, we did some elementary training and guard duty at Lester's Field and Petty Harbour.

Eventually we left Newfoundland and went to Ontario where we did further training. Next we went to England aboard the cruise ship *Orcades.* We were in a convoy, which was uneventful until we were off the coast Scotland, when the Spitfires came out to escort us in. By now we were getting news over the BBC. While in England, we did further training, but there was time for fun also. There were dances, leaves, and sightseeing in London and Scotland.

While preparing for the invasion, we did extensive training, which included schemes or mock battles. Another important aspect of our training was learning how to waterproof the tanks, which took place in Denoon, Scotland. On June 5, 1944, before we had a chance to load our LCT [landing craft tank], the invasion was postponed due to inclement weather. The next day we got the okay to go. While preparing to go and on the actual morning of the invasion, I was thinking what going into actual battle would be like, and if I was going to survive.

On June 6 we landed with the second wave on Juno Beach, and we advanced inland a few kilometers. The next day our troop was ordered to advance. There was a lot of heavy fighting one and a half miles west of the Abbey Ardennes. While in action, our gunner took out two Jerry tanks, but shortly after, we took an 88-mm shell in our engine compartment, and she went up in smoke. We had to bail out and we crawled to a wooded area, hoping to get back to our lines, which were approximately five kilometers back. After approximately half an hour in the wooded area, the 12th SS put in a counterattack and overtook our crew and two guys from B Squadron. We were all taken prisoner and marched to the Abbey Ardennes. While here we saw infantry that had been shot in cold blood. We were taken to a barn on the grounds of the abbey and lined up to be killed in cold blood like the others. Fortunately, before this came about, a senior officer came in and stopped him. They kept us there overnight, and in the morning they had us, about 100 prisoners in total, walk on the road to Rennes in southern France. This took approximately one week as it was 165 kilometers long, and en route we were strafed by two American Mustangs, killing several of our prisoners, until they realized who we were, and then they flew off doing the victory roll.

When we arrived at Rennes, we were all like a wet rag. We had very little to eat except the odd slice of black bread and some cabbage leaves from a farmer's field. We were there in a camp for approximately two weeks, and the Americans were closing in from the south. We were then loaded in boxcars, and it took 23 days to get to Germany, with a couple of stops in between. In July we were taken to a camp in Merseburg, and by September we were put in boxcars again for a trip to Leipzig, where a bunch of us were put in a gas works plant and taken out on work parties every morning. Once in a while we received Red Cross parcels, which made things more bearable.

In April 1945, when the Russians and Americans were closing in, they mustered every prisoner in the area and put us on a forced-route march going around in circles between the lines. On April 23 we were in this barn, and the guards had thrown away their weapons. They told us that there was a gap in the lines and that we were free to go, which we did. Sometime in the afternoon we reached the town of Wurgon, and the American front lines. We were free at last. When I entered captivity, I was 184 lbs., and when I was freed, I weighed 140 lbs. One other interesting note was that we saw the Americans and the Russians meet at the river Elbe. I was discharged on July 30, 1945.

Hubert Thistle lives in Scarborough, Ontario. □□

ARTHUR FREDERICK WHITE

DATE ENTERED SERVICE:
September 1941

CAMPAIGNS:
Northwest Europe

DECORATIONS:
Service Star 1939-1945, France and Germany Star, Defence of Britain, Canadian Volunteer Service Medal with clasp, Dutch Medal of Remembrance, Victory Medal

REGIMENT:
Sherbrooke Fusiliers, Regiment de Maisonneuve, 1st Canadian Armoured Carrier Regiment

SERIAL #: D47051

I was born St. John's, Newfoundland, on March 11, 1922, to Walter and Edith White. I grew up in the west end of the capital city on Leslie Street. Shortly after the war started I was interested in joining the army like my older brother Ron. He joined the 57th Newfoundland Royal Artillery, which later became the 166th. I could not join at this time because you had to be 21 years old and I was not interested in falsifying my birth certificate.

In 1941 I tried to get in the air force. I was even going around for a little while with an air force volunteer band on my arm. This did not materialize either, because I had a problem with my ear and I was told that I would not be able to fly more than 10,000 feet. After working for a period of time, I decided if I could not get in the British forces, I would try the Canadian.

At the age of 19, I went to Lester's Field in St. John's to join the Canadian Army. The Royal Rifles of Canada were there, but at the time that I was going to enlist, they had stopped recruiting. The recruiter said to come back in three weeks and we'll see then. I came back in three weeks and they were not there. The Sherbrooke Fusiliers were there instead, a rifle regiment. The Royal Rifles were gone on to Hong Kong. Now had I been accepted for the Royal Rifles, I could have been a prisoner of war or worse after the fall of Hong Kong.

I joined the army for three reasons. First of all, my older brother Ron was in the 57th Newfoundland Royal Artillery, which later became the 166th. I joined the army with the hope that I would meet up with my brother, and I got that chance in Salisbury Plain in England. Now the second incentive was, in those days, if you were not getting in something, the girls would consider you a slacker. There was always that there. The other reason, I would have to say, was the fact that I considered Hitler a monster. It looked as though, if he took over England, the next thing he would be over here. Everybody became patriotic. In addition to these reasons, all my friends were joining up.

Because the Canadian Army was accepting recruits at 19, I was accepted. I was given the opportunity to work in the orderly room as a clerk, but I did not want to be in Headquarters Squadron so I was put in one of the rifle sections. Not very long after, we started training. We were going around here to various places on guard like Portugal Cove, Topsail, and Petty Harbour. Then we started doing guard duty in the nighttime.

When we left Newfoundland, we went to a place called Debert, Nova Scotia. It was here that we changed from an infantry regiment to an armoured one. Those who did not wish to be part of an armoured regiment had the option of transferring to another infantry regiment. I loved this because I did not have a licence to drive a car as I was just out of school and had just started work. So I volunteered to be a tank driver. While here at Debert, I did a course as a driver-mechanic. From Debert we went over to England. It was here that I used to get a big wave from the 59th Newfoundland Royal Artillery as they would notice the Newfoundland badge on my arm.

In November 1943 I was in Christchurch, and I received word from my family that my brother had been killed in Italy. I carried on and in January 1944 I was out on a scheme, which is a mock battle. Somewhere on the way back to Christchurch, the tank that I was in broke down and another tank towed us with cross-tow cables that were crossed like an X. When he turned the corner to head down to Christchurch, one of the cables broke. As a result, the tank that was towing went in the drain. I jumped out to take up the slack in the cable, thinking that he was going to back up and come out of the drain. Instead of that he went ahead. The cable came taut, banged me in the legs and knocked me down. I was crouched over and the track came up on me. It pushed my arm into my stomach and twisted it around. It came on my hip and fractured my pelvis on both sides. I was fortunate that the guy driving the tank put on the brakes because another inch and I would not be here today. They put me on a stretcher, and along came an officer and asked me if I wanted a cigarette. This was the last thing that I wanted.

As a result of this accident, I spent five months in total in a hospital in Christchurch. Here I was, on my back, dealing with the loss of my brother and my accident. I was also concerned about worrying my parents, so I wrote home and told them that I had a little argument with a tank and was writing this letter on my back in a hospital. This worried them more than anything. They did not know if I was dying as well.

While in hospital, I had to learn to walk all over again. Once I could walk, I went to Aldershot. While there, I was working in the kitchen and out in the parade ground doing rifle drill. Now for me, doing rifle drill was fine, but when I ordered arms, the rifle would go bang off the ground. They sent me for an examination, and I said to the doctor, "Look, I didn't spend all this time to quit." He gave me three options: you can go home, stay here and work in the kitchen and out in the parade square, or we will take you if you want.

I chose the third option and I promised him I would never drive a tank again. I had to admit that I couldn't drive a tank like previously. The reason was that a tank was not like a car where you can steer with a steering wheel. In a tank you have two tiller bars, one on the left and one on the right. When you pull on the left tiller bar, it stops the boogey wheels and you go around on your left. When you pull on the right ones, it stops on the right-hand side and you go around on your right. When you pull on two of them, you stop. I had no strength in my left arm. So I would have to take the tiller bar and put my leg around it to pull it back. It was the same for the other side. As a result I promised the doctor that I would be a co-driver and fire the machine gun. I would only drive in case of an emergency, like if the driver was killed or wounded.

I then went from my armoured regiment, the Sherbrooke Fusiliers, to a new regiment that was made. This regiment was formed out of people who came from North Africa, Sicily, Italy, and from all over Canada. For one reason or another they came on through. We all went in this new regiment, and it was called the First Canadian Armoured Carrier Regiment. Our new regiment used improvised Ram tanks, which are those with the turret removed so that there was room for the driver and the co-driver. They then had enough room to carry 16 infantrymen into battle and drop them off at the first business. They jumped out and started fighting. The name that got pinned on the regiment and never lost was the "Kangaroo Regiment." On my cap badge is a kangaroo. This is what we did. We went forward with the infantry, dropped them off on the outskirts of a village, and they went into battle. We went back, took another 16, went right on through while the fighting was going on, to the next stop. Here I was, I went to this regiment, and they came from everywhere, and it was a laughing stock, Kangaroo Regiment. In fact, some of those who came did not want to come at all.

I went from England to Belgium up to Nijmegen, Holland, and we were there for a while until we got organized. I came up as part of reinforcements. My first bit of action was on the outskirts of Holland, and it was in the middle of a blinding snowstorm. When I was in action, I did not know what was coming, but a good shot of grog did something or other. It was pure stuff.

We passed through some POW camps. Yes, I remember it well, what the Germans did. Psychologically they had it all figured out. They took our guys and put them over where the Russians and Poles would be freeing them, and they put the Russians in our area. As a result, when we were liberating camps, we were freeing Russians and Poles.

Another aspect that comes to mind was the SS. They took 65-year-old men, and boys aged 12, put them up against us. They turned the gun on them and forced them to fight. They would stick them up there when they got short. These things stick in your mind.

I remember several times we would be sitting on the back of a tank playing cards, with shells whizzing around, but you get immune.

I was also involved in the Battle of the Bulge, which is on the Rhine River. From there we went into Germany. On VE-Day, I was in Germany playing football [soccer] when they came around and told us that the war was over. I came home on the same ship that I went over on, the *Queen Elizabeth*, with 6000 servicemen on board. We came through New York and up through Montreal. I was in Camphill Hospital in Halifax where I was discharged.

Arthur White lives in St. John's. □□

WILLIAM ALEXANDER LUSCOMBE

DATE ENTERED SERVICE:
November 1942

CAMPAIGNS:
Northwest Europe

DECORATIONS:
Service Star 1939-1945, France and Germany Star, Defence of Britain, Canadian Volunteer Service Medal with clasp, Victory Medal, Dutch Medal of Remembrance

REGIMENT:
Royal Canadian Engineers, Canadian Infantry Corps, North Nova Scotia Highlanders

SERIAL #: F91309

I was born on July 8, 1925, to John and Clara Luscombe in St. John's. I went to school at Prince of Wales and Bishop Feild, and I was also in the CLB [Church Lads Brigade] bugle band and played the bugle and drums. With the outbreak of the war in 1939 I was only 14 years old. One night after band practice when I was 16 years old, my friend, Carl Ennis, and another fella, Drover, approached me to inform me that they were going to Lester's Field in the morning to join up with the Royal Rifles of Canada. He said we were going to be okay because we were going to be in the band, and that the band does not get involved in the fighting. What he didn't know at the time was that the band would serve as stretcher-bearers, which was very dangerous. He joined with the Drover chap, and I changed my mind at that time. Unfortunately, they went on and became prisoners of war for quite a long time and suffered greatly.

All my good friends were in the service, and every time I would see them they would be in uniform. There was a lot of excitement about being in the army, and of course the girls all went for the guys in uniform. In November 1942, at the age of 17, I enlisted in the Canadian Army with my friend Bill Gruchy. We thought we were going to join the Lincoln Wellington Regiment, but they were not taking recruits so instead we joined the Royal Canadian Engineers.

During the month of December, I was still not in uniform. On the night of December 12, 1942, Bill Gruchy and I were at the CLB Armoury playing pool at the Old Comrades Club. All of a sudden someone rushed in and said, "The K of C [Knights of Columbus hostel] is on fire," which was right next door. We rushed out and the flames were coming out. There were very few people coming out of there, and Bill Ivany happened to be one of them. I remember he was all blackened from the smoke. I mentioned to him after, but he could not remember me with all the excitement and everything. We stayed there and the cars and buses were stopping to put people in and take them to the hospital.

My service record shows that I served in Canada, the North Atlantic area, the United Kingdom, and continental Europe. In January 1943, after receiving a release from the Newfoundland government, I was sworn in as a sapper with the Royal Canadian Engineers. I had to give my age as 19 in order to be accepted. At first I was stationed up in Lester's Field, and because I did not have a trade, they put me to work in the stores. I later got transferred to Botwood to work at the powerhouse to provide electricity for the two army camps, the airport, and the hospital.

In the spring of 1944, I received notification that I was being reallocated to the infantry, to the Canadian Infantry Corps, which was another branch of the Canadian armed services. I was sent to Debert and Windsor, Nova Scotia, where I did infantry training. I was then put on a draft for overseas and went to Halifax to board the troopship *Aquitania* that carried between 10-15 thousand troops. We set sail for the United Kingdom, and after thirteen days at sea, with the daily threat of U-boats, we eventually landed in the seaport of Gourock in Scotland. From there we went on to Aldershot for more training. We then went to New Haven near Brighton in southern England, and there we boarded LCIs [landing craft infantry], crossed the English Channel and landed in Dieppe, France, where I was attached to the North Nova Scotia Highlanders as a reinforcement to replace the boys who had been killed or wounded. The North Nova Scotia Highlanders were part of the 9th Canadian Highland Infantry Brigade in the 3rd Canadian Infantry Division.

We proceeded on up through France and then to Ghent in Belgium. We crossed the Leopold Canal aboard the buffalos [amphibious troop carriers] and landed on the banks of the Scheldt Estuary. Our objective was Breskens and it was one of the toughest battles of the war for Canadians. There were many casualties. We later went to the border of Holland and Germany to relieve the 101st American Airborne Division that had just previously made a landing by gliders and parachutes in the area of Gros Beek. That was exciting because we were no more than two or three hundred yards away from the Germans. We did a lot of fighting patrols and raids in this area, taking prisoners to find out what German units we would be facing. It was all dyke country. We took over the front line at Gros Beek. We later moved on into Germany and fought our way along, preparing for the Rhine crossing. The North Novas, as they were called, went across the Rhine, landing at a place called Beinen, where very heavy fighting took place with many casualties, killed and wounded. From there the North Novas started the long trek up through northern Holland, liberating the Dutch people as they went.

The infantry soldiers were the ones who did the fighting. All other units supported the infantry. That is not to say that others never saw any action, because they did, especially the tank corps. When they were called on, they came in support of the infantry. We had to move ahead by foot and take all the hidden objectives. Life was not always that pleasant as an infantry soldier. We faced the challenges of the weather and the enemy. There was the zoom boom of the 88-mm gun [anti-tank, anti-aircraft], the demoralizing sound of the moaning minnies, land mines, booby traps, machine-gun fire, airburst shells that exploded over your head, just to mention a few things. The army food was good while in training, but while in action in the front lines, it was meat and vegetables, which we would eat cold out of the can. It was not very good but it was something nourishing. Sometimes we would have to go without food for short periods due to the fighting conditions.

After being in action for a period of time, you were entitled to a leave. The only other way to get out when the war was on was to get injured or killed. Throughout the war I was a private, and I didn't want to be anything else, because the higher up you went, this increased the chances of you being killed. There was no trouble of moving up in rank because quite often you were the oldest-serving man in the platoon. My total time served was three years, two months. Within that time period, I spent almost eighteen months as an infantry soldier with the North Nova Scotia Highlanders, including eight months in action in the front lines.

After the war ended, we stayed in Holland in a town called Zeist near Utrecht until December 1945 when we were shipped back to England. Eventually we boarded the *Duchess of Bedford* in Liverpool and sailed for Canada. It took twelve days through rough seas in which many were seasick. We arrived at St. John's to let a number of British war brides disembark. Even though there were quite a few Newfoundlanders on board, we were not permitted to leave the ship as we were part of the Canadian Army. I was discouraged and disappointed at the time because it was between Christmas and New

Year's and everybody was celebrating, especially with the troops coming home. Due to bad weather we had to stay for 48 hours before leaving for Halifax.

We arrived there a few days later in the wee hours of the morning, into Halifax Harbour to the sounds of the bagpipes that were beaming. There was a great reception at the Sports Arena, which was very exciting and emotional. We then came across country by train. Every place we stopped the people were giving us goodies. They were very kind to us.

We were given thirty days' leave to go home to our families, and then return to Halifax, where I was discharged in February 1946. On the way home I met my wife-to-be while sailing on the SS *Kyle* across the Gulf of St. Lawrence. She was also a member of the Canadian Army.

Nobody knows what the infantry soldiers had to put up with, only they, themselves, and they don't talk about it because it brings back too many bad memories. So I won't go into the gory details, but I will say that war is an awful thing and it left scars on all of those who served in the front lines. We had the toughest job because when we went in there, we stayed in there. We were being shot at night and day. It was non-stop. My regiment suffered almost 500 killed and, I believe, thousands wounded during the eleven months from D-Day, June 6, 1944, to May 8, 1945.

The following article was written by Bill Luscombe in 2003:

> *My view from a slit trench...remembering the Battle of the Scheldt, Belgium and Holland, October 1944.*
>
> *How do you describe the physical pain, the mental pain of a teenaged infantry soldier who used to dream of adventure and excitement and who now exists in a hole in the ground known as a slit trench (approximately four feet long, 20-24" wide, and four feet deep) in a foreign country far away from home? Your feet are submerged in the icy-cold muddy water, and the pouring rain*

makes your already drenched body shake and tremble. Your wet and muddy uniform sticks to your flesh. You wonder how long you can absorb this punishment hour after hour, day after day. You long for some badly needed sleep. The constant smell, the awful odour of the battlefield and the stench of the dead bodies, is all around you.

The days are long, the nights are longer, and you think to yourself, How come I am doing this? And you think again of your warm, cozy bed back home where all is so peaceful. But you must face reality and you are where you are and there is no way out except to catch an enemy bullet or a chunk of hot shrapnel and be lucky enough then to make it out of there without getting hit again. Or perhaps the big one might get you and blow you to kingdom come.

On the mental side of it, you wonder how long you can survive the never-ending saga, the zoom boom of the 88-mm, the no-warning German shell, the demoralizing sound of the moaning minnies, the big freight-train shell that you hear coming your way. It's going to be a close one, then the airburst shells explode overhead, sending shrapnel down on you.

You are always waiting to hear the words "prepare to move," which may come at any time during the day or night. It usually means that once again you go on the attack. The artillery starts and if it's daytime and the weather is good, you may suddenly hear the Typhoons approaching. The tiffies, as we called them, carried six rockets, three on each wing. As you move ahead, you always fear, apart from the enemy fire, the thought of the tiffie rockets exploding much too close up in front of you or the friendly fire, our own artillery shells falling short, which happened quite often, then the constant machine-gun fire. And there was the German smizer machine gun known as the "burp" gun; one burp could mean a hundred or more rounds heading your way. Another threat as you move ahead is the land mines. You know that every step you take you could be ruined for life if you get hit in a vital spot.

If you reach your objective, once again you dig in and you are back in your hole in the ground and the mortar shells are coming awful close. The Germans are masters with the mortar. There is just no rest and it starts all over again. By this time, you feel hungry, so you open up another can of M & V, meat and vegetables, and it tastes the same as the one before, cold and greasy. Maybe later, when things quiet down a bit, you hope for a bit of sleep. And so it goes.

Bill Luscombe resides in St. John's with his wife Vicki Goodyear Luscombe, who is also a veteran of World War II. Her story appears on page 70. □□

CARL STEWARD RENDELL

DATE ENTERED SERVICE:
March 1943

CAMPAIGNS:
Northwest Europe

DECORATIONS:
1939-1945 Star, Canadian Volunteer Service Medal and clasp, Victory Medal, Defence Medal, France and Germany Star, Dutch Medal, Volunteer Korean Medal, United Nations Medal

REGIMENT:
Royal Canadian Engineers (5th Fortress Company), North Shore (New Brunswick) Regiment, R.C.E.M.E.

SERIAL #: F91318

I was born on December 9, 1923, to Chesley H. and Helena J. Rendell in Rattling Brook, near King's Point in Green Bay, Newfoundland. I went to school in Corner Brook. My brother Chesley, who was three and a half years older than I, went overseas on June 5, 1940, with the 59th [Newfoundland Heavy Regiment Royal Artillery]. I was secretly hoping that the war would last long enough until I was old enough to go, although I did not want to see any more killing.

I met a fella in Corner Brook, Harvey Dewey, who was from St. John's. He was working there and we became friends. When I came to St. John's, I looked Harvey up, and he wanted to join the armed forces also. We tried the air force, but my eyesight was not good enough, and Dewey was also turned down. We then went to Lester's Field to join up. We had to get permission from the colonel of the Newfoundland Militia Regiment, and then we were accepted into the engineers.

While here in Newfoundland, we did very little training. We worked at erecting Nissan huts, and we also camouflaged the lighthouse out at Fort Amherst. Harold Cahill, Harv Dewey, and I had to stick a little ladder out on the side of a cliff, on a little ledge. Two guys held on to the ladder while one painted. It was a scary job because when you looked down, all you saw were the waves bashing up against the rock.

We left Newfoundland and went to Windsor, Nova Scotia, where we did some basics. Then in 1944 we were transferred to Debert, Nova Scotia, for some final infantry training. We trained there for about six weeks. We went overseas on the *Aquitania* and landed in Scotland. We stayed there overnight and then they shipped us by train through London to Aldershot. On D-Day I was home in Corner Brook for de-embarkation leave.

Shortly after, I returned and was shipped over to Dieppe, France, where we were at an A Echelon for a while, which is a forward group. Then we were all separated because it went by the initial of your surname. Bill Luscombe went to the North Nova Scotia Highlanders, and I went with the next group, which was the North Shore [New Brunswick] Regiment. This is how we were separated. We were in the same division, but he was in the 9th Brigade and I was in the 8th Brigade. The 8th consisted of the North Shore [New Brunswick] Regiment, the Chaudiere Regiment, which was French Canadian, and the Queen's Own Rifles. We went through France with just about no opposition except for the border between Belgium and Germany. We were mobile in trucks.

Our first action was the Scheldt Estuary, which was quite a do. We crossed in those motorized amphibious vehicles, like tanks, but they were amphibious. We crossed through the Scheldt and we were there about six weeks. I am not sure. This was a very difficult campaign. The Scheldt was a water battle. You would dig a slit trench and before you would get down six inches it would start to fill up with water. If it didn't fill up with water, it would rain. They were cold, wet, and damp conditions. The food was another thing. If you had a cast-iron stomach, you might be able to endure it. You would open a tin of meat and vegetable stew, and there would be fat on it an inch thick. Then you had to eat it cold. Once in a while the cooker, which was normally back at headquarters of the company, would come forward with a hot meal.

In some places we had stiff opposition, especially from the Hitler Youth or the paratroopers. Other times we would be up against old home guard fellas in the tail end of it. Our intelligence would let us know whom we were battling. After the Scheldt we came back to Ghent for a three-day recreational leave, and then we joined our regiment getting ready to cross the Rhine. I think it was April 8, 1945, when we crossed the Rhine. We fought in various towns and cities in Germany like Emmerich. We would take a town and then bivouac there overnight in whatever we could find, like a slit trench or an old barn. Then we went to Nijmegen, which had already been taken, but we were stationed along the banks of the River Waal. We saw a bit of action here, even though the city had been taken as there were pockets of German resistance.

I remember being in action, and we would put down a yellow flag so that our own aircraft fighters could identify us. A lot of times the flag was not down properly, either it blew away or they just did not see it. Sometimes we were strafed by Typhoons, which were our own aircraft. You would be sitting down in the slit trench and you would see the Typhoons coming. They would release their rockets when it seemed like two miles away from you. These rockets would then land over you or near you. I saw lots of fellas out in an old trench or a ditch, in front of our slit trench having a crap. When the Typhoons would come, you would see them run to the slit trench with their pants half down.

When the war ended, I was in a little town called Stracholt, which was near Emden in northwest Germany. I was discharged in 1945, and in 1947, I enlisted again. In the interim after the war I did a machinist course in Hamilton, Ontario. I was in Korea from 1953-1954. This time, instead of going in the infantry, I was with RCEME, that is, Royal Canadian Electrical Mechanical Engineering, which was attached to the British Royal Engineers. I was driving around in a mobile machine shop. The engineers would call up and say, for example, that the tractor has slipped a pin or something. We would make a pin to fit it and deliver it. I was there for one year, and by the time I got there, the truce was started. When I got home from Korea, I met my wife, and she did not want any part of the army.

Last Memorial Day a guy said to me, "Ah, here comes a hero." I said, "I was no hero, but I was no coward either." If I was a young man, I would do it all over again.

Carl Rendell passed away on July 6, 2006. □□

Trafalgar Square 1945
Left to Right: Bill Luscombe and John Hicks.
Kneeling: Carl Rendell.

HAROLD LAWRENCE CAHILL

DATE ENTERED SERVICE:
November 9, 1942

CAMPAIGNS:
Northwest Europe

DECORATIONS:
Service Star 1939-1945, France and Germany Star, Defence of Britain, Canadian Volunteer Service Medal and clasp, The War Medal, Canadian Centennial Medal, Long Service Commissioners, Canadian Forces Decoration, Dutch Liberation Medal

REGIMENT:
Royal Canadian Engineers (5th Fortress Company), Royal Canadian Artillery, Royal Hamilton Light Infantry, North Nova Scotia Highlanders

SERIAL #: F91312

I was born on November 14, 1923, in St. John's to Michael and Mary Edith Cahill. During my childhood I grew up on Theatre Hill, and in 1935 we moved to Franklyn Avenue. I attended school at St. Bon's.

Fred Evans and I went to Lester's Field to join the Canadian Army. In order to join we had to get permission from the Commission of Government. I had to get a letter from the Honourable L.E. Emerson, who was the Minister of Justice. We had to produce this before they let us go in. When we joined, we became Canadian citizens. I joined the army because everyone else was joining and I wasn't going to stay home by myself. I picked the Royal Canadian Engineers because most of my friends were in it already.

We did some training here in St. John's, but there was not much to it. We did a lot of drill, and learned how to use a rifle, but for the most part there was very little basic training. I started with the 5th Fortress Company, which later became the 16th E.S. and W. Company, Engineers, Service, and Works Company. We did all the works of the base at Lester's Field. Then we transferred to Mundy Pond where the present-day Purity Factories in St. John's are located. While here, we were looking after all the weapons and everything else. I was with the camouflage and bomb disposal sections.

On December 12, 1942, the K of C [Knights of Columbus] hostel in St. John's burned down, with the loss of 99 people along with several hurt. My father, who was one of the inspectors for the Newfoundland Constabulary, was one of the people investigating the cause of the fire. The Royal Canadian Engineers, which I was part of, had the task of removing the bodies out of the rubble. Around this time there were a number of suspicious fires. The week before there had been one at Chain Rock, and toilet paper was found ready to be lit in the Red Triangle Club on Water Street.

I was also part of constructing the dummy guns at Cape Spear, along with my friends Bill Luscombe and Harvey Dewey. When that was finished, I ended up in Windsor, Nova Scotia, where the personnel selection officer put us into groups. We were not there that long and we ended up in Petawawa, Ontario, for the 1st Engineers. I was selected to do my engineer's training while my friends were transferred to the infantry. While here, I learned my specialty, which was mines and booby traps. I also learned bridging, which was all learned in a five-week course. Upon completion of the engineer's course, I finished tops in my class. They wanted to keep me on as an instructor, but I told them that I did not join the army to stay in Petawawa. They gave into my whims at the time and transferred me to the Potential Driver Operator Artillery, which was located in Borden, England. Before going to England I was given a 48-hour leave to go home.

We ended up in Grennoch, Scotland, and from there we took a train down to Borden. While there, I started off on the 25-pounders but I was only there a couple of days. Then I was sent down to do some signal training, and I became a signal operator. When I completed this course, I returned to Aldershot. Shortly after, I was put in a holding station and when the time came to go, I ended up with the Royal Hamilton Light Infantry, which was more commonly known as the Rileys.

We landed at the port of Cherbourg, which was part of Juno Beach. This was not on June 6, 1944, but it was within the month of June. We arrived on the beach and the boys were farther inland. Now there was still lots of stuff falling behind the fellas that were inland. We did not see any action until we got farther inland, but you did see what happened. You would then say a few prayers. I was part of the infantry and I was a Bren gunner. First going in was very rough, but it became a day's work. Sometimes you would get bogged down for a while and you would start to think. Other times you had to dig a slit trench very fast. Every day was a close call. I always looked at it, if my time had come, I was going to get it.

We liberated Caen but the biggest battle was Carpiquet. We were there for days, battling back and forth, back and forth. Another battle was Falaise where we lost a lot of good men, and that was the hardest part. We then went up through the Scheldt in Belgium, which involved more heavy fighting. In fact, I was just outside Nijmegen when the battle of Arnhem was on. We were at a place called Gros Beek Hill in Holland that today we call Glider Hill. This is where the gliders came in and a lot of them crashed with quite a few men getting killed. While in Holland, we were into the water fighting.

We went up through Nijmegen and came back through Nijmegen and proceeded up through Germany in a place called Krannenberg. This is where I came down with bronchial pneumonia. In spite of this I crossed the Rhine at Wesel with a temperature of 102 degrees with a Bren gun on my shoulder. We walked seven kilometers. We got into a barn and I slept there all night until the next morning when they put me in the hospital. The war was over for me at that time. That was April 1, 1945. At the end of April I came out of the hospital and then I went to a convalescent place for a few days. Next, I had a leave and I ended up in Scotland for a few days. When I returned to Ghent, Belgium, I went into a holding area to see where they were going to put me. While there, I saw my buddies, Dewey and Lusc, on their way back from leave. They said, "Why don't you come with us?" And this is what I did. They were with the North Nova Scotia Highlanders. I was discharged on February 23, 1946, as a private.

I loved my time in the military and I got called back on continuous military service on October 22, 1956. I went in the engineers again here in St. John's. I took over the complete administration for the Canadian Army and Militia. On November 19, 1968, I was discharged as an RSM, a regimental sergeant major in administration. Today I am supervisor of the commissioners at the RCMP building. I am the only war veteran left in the commissioners in Newfoundland.

Harold Cahill has since retired and lives in Mount Pearl. □□

WILLIAM GARLAND IVANY

DATE ENTERED SERVICE:
October 10, 1942

CAMPAIGNS:
Northwest Europe

DECORATIONS:
Canadian Volunteer Service Medal, 1939-1945 Star, Victory Medal, France and Germany Star, Defence Medal, Dutch Medal of Remembrance

REGIMENT: Royal Canadian Engineers

SERIAL #: F91305

I was born on September 7, 1925, in Harbour Grace to Simeon and Annie Ivany. A few months after I was born, we moved to St. John's. When the war broke out I was attending school at Holy Cross. After I finished school, I had an opportunity to work with a chartered accountant. I was supposed to start on a Monday, but this never happened because I joined the army on Friday. At the age of 17, I went to Lester's Field to join the Canadian Army. Originally, I was interested in the air force but the age restrictions were quite heavy. It seemed that the Canadian Army was not as strict on age requirements. There were a lot of people joining so I went with the flow.

After joining the army in October, my career almost came to an abrupt end on December 12, 1942. My friend John O'Flaherty and I went to the K of C [Knights of Columbus hostel] that night and luckily we did not have any ladies with us. There was so much confusion, and if I had lost my date, I would have felt terrible. I remember we were sitting down watching the stage show when all of a sudden the lights went out and then somebody yelled fire. Oh, gee whizzes, it was chaos, and with the lights out, you did not know where to go or what to do. I think I made my way up toward the stage, put a curtain around my face, or one of those stage things. Then a funny thing happened. I felt a bit of fresh air, and this must have been where the door was open and the air was coming in. Naturally, I headed toward where the air was coming, but before I got to the door it went up in flames. Then I had the choice of either staying or going through the fire. I decided to go through it and this is how I got my hands and face burnt. Luckily I was wearing my great coat, which was made of a very heavy woolen material. That saved my body from getting the flash of the burn.

Another thing I remember, and I am not sure if there was any truth to it, but they say that there was nobody got out of the K of C after the fire trucks came. Now when I came through the door, I tripped over a fire hose. There was nobody behind me, so I don't know if I was the last one out or not. *

Once out of the building, they put us on a bus and drove us to St. Clare's Hospital. When I arrived there, I was mobile and they were not paying too much attention to walking casualties.

As a result I got a ride over to the Grace Hospital, which was closer to my home on Campbell Avenue. After leaving the Grace, I walked in my house and my mother fainted because I was all black. Then they called my aunt, who was a nurse, for assistance. She came and put some gunk on my face and so forth. The next morning the ambulance came and brought me to Lester's Field. I spent a month in hospital and another month or so recuperating from various burns. My friend John O'Flaherty also survived the fire.

During my service in Newfoundland, I was stationed at Lester's Field and Winterholme, which was an office building in St. John's for the Canadian Army. In November 1943 I was sent to an army camp in Kentville, Nova Scotia. We did some training here and on December 23, we were shipped to Halifax on a troop ship called *Ile de France.* On the way over, my claim to fame was that I was in charge of the detail for cleaning up the ships. There were a lot of people getting sick on the way over, and I did not have to do any of the dirty work.

We landed in Liverpool on New Year's Day 1944, and shortly after I arrived, they took away my rank of lance-corporal, which I received six months before. In the army they have an establishment for so many sergeants, corporals, and lance-corporals, and I guess they were one over for lance-corporals.

In January 1944, we were switched down to Aldershot where I did a few months training. We were doing some basic training because I had only joined the army and I was not what you would call trained. One part of the training was where they would have a trench in the shape of an X. They would shove a grenade in one end, and you had to make sure you made it out the other. After we left Aldershot, we went to Surrey. From there we were going to ship out to Normandy in the month of July 1944. Then we had a change of orders and they whisked us back to England. Apparently, there were too many people in Normandy and they hadn't taken enough ground. I had said good-bye to my wife-to-be, and there I was, four days later, back again.

Finally, we went over to Normandy to a port called Arromanches. Then we were on the coast of Normandy. I am not sure how long we were there, but I know we were trying to take Caen for a long time. We then made our way up through France. We didn't meet any opposition but no doubt there was. As we were going through, things were starting to clear. I was not in the actual fighting. I was on guard duty and I drove officers to different places. I remember one time, and I was driving this officer in Germany, close to Bremen. This MP stopped us and asked us where we were going. We said, "We are going up to inspect this bridge."

He said, "No, you're not." We said, "Why not?" He said, "About three miles up the road are German soldiers." I remember another time in my career when my friend and I were looking for a transfer to the infantry. We were told that the army tells us where to go. The infantry was the roughest part of the whole operation.

After France, we made our way through Holland. What sticks out in my mind was that the people in Holland were actually starving. They were starving to the point where they would come and get the food that was dumped in the garbage containers. They would go through that and get what they needed. It was really heartbreaking.

When the hostilities ended in Europe, I was in Hilversam, Holland. From there I was transferred to London, where I was stationed between six and eight months. When I left London, I came home. Once home there were no major adjustments for me, but there were a few minor ones. When you left home, things were one way, and when you returned, things were another. In addition, I was recently married to my English girlfriend and I was looking for a job. If I had to do it all over again, I would.

Bill Ivany lives in St. John's. □□

* It should be noted that Edward Whelan, the head of the Criminal Investigation Division (CID), testified that at 11:15 the K of C was past redemption and there could be no chance of anybody surviving. The fire trucks were at the scene by 11:18. As Bill Ivany was a survivor of the fire, his eyewitness account sheds some new light on the K of C fire.

JOSEPH HARVEY DEWEY

DATE ENTERED SERVICE:
March 1943

CAMPAIGNS:
Battle of the Scheldt

DECORATIONS:
Service Star 1939-45, France and Germany Star, Defence of Britain, Canadian Volunteer Service Medal with clasp, Dutch Liberation Medal, Victory Medal

REGIMENT:
Royal Canadian Engineers, North Nova Scotia Highlanders

SERIAL #: F91317

I was born on August, 26, 1922, in St. John's to William James Dewey and Meta Clarke. As a child, I grew up on Monroe Street and Kitchener Avenue, and I spent some time in Corner Brook. I was called after my uncle, Joseph Dewey, who served in the Royal Newfoundland Regiment during World War One. Unfortunately, he died as a result of his wounds just three weeks before the end of hostilities. I attended school at Prince of Wales and played soccer and hockey. I excelled at both but I have been told that I could have played soccer on a professional level. After I completed school, I went to work at the American base at Fort Pepperrell.

At the age of 21, I enlisted in the Royal Canadian Engineers at Lester's Field in St. John's. I joined because I felt a sense of patriotism. I picked the army because my friends Bill Luscombe and Harold Cahill had joined. Shortly after we left Newfoundland, we went to Nova Scotia. While there, I was transferred to the infantry. My new regiment was the North Nova Scotia Highlanders. We did about six months of basic training, which included small arms, rifle range, grenades, and Bren gun. Once our training was complete, we were shipped overseas aboard the *Aquitania.* We landed in Liverpool, and then we went to Aldershot. We did some further training and eventually we went to France in July 1944. At this time there were still pockets of resistance in France. I remember walking up to this farmhouse and three bodies were covered in a brown blanket. We were there to take their place as we were the replacements.

My first experience with combat was in France. I was in a slit trench with a guy named Smokie. The mortar shells were coming in and he was shaking like a leaf. I was looking at him and I was not scared at all. I was a greenhorn, too green to be scared. After leaving France, we made our way to Holland. This led to a fierce battle, the battle for the Scheldt Estuary. This occurred through October and early November of 1944. While there, it rained all the time. The conditions were very wet. The Germans were really tough and they used to shell us all the time with their 88's and mortars.

When in combat on the front lines, we were about 300 feet away from the enemy. With regards to the food, sometimes it was scarce and you might not eat for two or three days. At other times, meals were prepared in field kitchens, called big dixies. In addition to this, we had emergency rations in the shape of a bar, and if you broke out the seal before you were supposed to, you would be charged. I recall during the night they would come around with a hot toddy. I wouldn't take mine. I would take a chocolate bar instead.

After the Scheldt, we went through Holland. I remember one day. We went up to the German border a short way from Holland. We were in a single file on our way to a farmhouse. In front of me was a Sergeant Lorne Russell from Victoria. In came a mortar shell, landed and exploded, and he fell down right in front of me. He gave a little quiver and he was dead.

Another aspect of Holland was when the Germans broke the dykes and all the land was flooded. Walking down the trail, the water was up to my waist, and this was cold.

On December 16, 1944, the Germans went on a major offensive in the Ardennes area. This became known as the Battle of the Bulge. We had heard that the Germans had overrun the Americans and killed a lot of them. There were even Germans in American uniforms to add to the confusion. When we went to the American lines, there were so many US soldiers shot and killed. At night there was a really heavy snowfall, and I was on guard duty that night when an officer came by and said, "Be on your guard, the Germans have overrun the Americans." On a better note, we had a good Christmas dinner that night, a turkey with all the trimmings. When my turn came, I went and had my meal. The Germans were eventually beaten back and I spent the remainder of the war in Holland. As I became more experienced in combat, I was frightened to death. I thought I was going to be killed for sure. When I was going into battle, I would recite, "Yea, though I walk through the valley of the shadow of death, I fear no evil, for thou are with me, thy rod and thy staff comfort me."

I remember being in Holland just before Christmas. We were in a field with very tall grass. The Germans were raking through it with machine-gun fire. You could hear swish, swish, the bullets flying through the grass. There was a lieutenant there and it was his first day there. The officer stood up and asked the Germans to surrender, and they shot him right on the spot. He fell down. He was dead. Eventually, we made our way back to the farmhouse, and a parcel had arrived addressed to this man who had just been killed. It was from his wife. One of the byes asked, "Will we open it?" We said, "Yes." We opened it up and there was a small note there. "My Dear Darling, here is something to keep you nice and warm." Here was a sweater she had knitted for her husband and he had just been killed.

I recall in Holland we were at a submarine base and there were German soldiers there. There were some young Dutch girls who were fraternizing with the enemy. They took them out in the town where they came from, and they paraded them through the streets, naked, with their heads shaved. They then whipped them with purses.

When the war ended, we were still in Holland. They gave us a bottle of beer each. The war was over on May 8, 1945, but I did not arrive home until December 29, 1945. I came home on the *Duchess of Bedford.* If things were the same again, I think I would do it all over again.

Harv Dewey lives in Topsail. □□

EMILY VICTORIA GOODYEAR [LUSCOMBE]

DATE ENTERED SERVICE:
July 1943

DECORATIONS:
Canadian Volunteer Service Medal, 1939-1945 Star, Victory Medal

REGIMENT: Canadian Women's Army Corps

SERIAL #: W60292

DRAFT: 1st

I was born on July 16, 1925, in St. John's to Val and Elsie Goodyear. I went to school at St. Thomas and I went to work at the Royal stores in 1942. At the age of sixteen I tried to join the air force, but I was too young. At the age of eighteen I enlisted in the Canadian Army. It was an exciting time, and it seemed like the thing to do. This was a really happy time for me but not my mother. She was really upset with me. She had my brother Tom in the Merchant Navy and she had lost a brother in the First World War. And going on a ship at that time, with the *Caribou* sinking a couple of years before, it was dangerous. When you are young, you do not think of things like that.

I left St. John's on the *Fort Amherst* on August 2, 1943, and we went to Halifax. During this time there was a blackout, of course, and the ship was blacked out as well. I was sworn in in Halifax and went to Kitchener, Ontario, and did a basic training and a driver's course. Each course lasted six weeks. After my training I was stationed in Chilliwack, British Columbia, where I was a driver. I was there for a year and then I went to Vancouver, where I was for the remainder of the war. I was able to return home for a two-week leave, and it took me eleven days to get home from BC by train. By the time I arrived home, I had tonsilitis and I was in bed for a couple of weeks. After my leave I went back to Vancouver in a bomber, and I remember it being so cold.

I loved my time in the army, and when it came time to be discharged, we drew straws, because among the eight of us who were dispatch drivers, not one of us wanted to leave. It wasn't all party but I really enjoyed what I was doing. At that time there were very few women driving, and to get a driver's licence and drive was fantastic. I used to work for everyone else. If someone wanted a night off, I would do the shift. I was discharged in February 1946.

Vicki Luscombe resides in St. John's with her husband William, who is also a veteran. His story appears on page 46. □□

Emily Goodyear [Luscombe] drives her military vechicle through Vancouver on August 15, 1945, as civilians and military personnel celebrate the end of World War II.

CHAPTER 2

ROYAL CANADIAN AIR FORCE WOMEN'S DIVISION

In May 1942 recruiters from the RCAF Women's Division came to Newfoundland. They went to St. John's, Grand Falls and Corner Brook. All together, 260 young women were accepted. The majority went to Toronto for their basic training. When that was complete, they were split up and assigned to various RCAF stations to begin their work as clerk stenographers or in clerk operations.

JESSIE WINDSOR [GOODYEAR]

DATE ENTERED SERVICE:
June 1942

DECORATIONS:
1939-1945 Canadian Volunteer Service Medal with bar, Victory Medal

REGIMENT: RCAFWD

SERIAL #: W305136

I was born on September 25, 1920, to Stanley and Mary Dixon Windsor. I was educated at Bishop Spencer College on Bond Street in St. John's. Before the war, I worked as a stenographer at Government House and later at Fort Pepperrell.

I was one of the first from Newfoundland to enlist in the women's division of the air force, and I did so because I felt that I should. I did my basic training in Toronto and I was then sent to Calgary for recruiting and was promoted to corporal. While there, my brother Bill, who was coming home on his first leave from the Royal Navy, was lost when the *Caribou* was sunk by a German U-boat on October 14, 1942. While in Calgary, I applied for overseas. They did post me overseas, which was

Torbay, Newfoundland. At the time, Newfoundland was a country and a colony of Britain. While at Torbay, I worked at administration in the orderly room, which was at the main office. In April 1943 I was married to Tom Goodyear, who was in the Merchant Navy.

Jessie Windsor Goodyear lives in St. John's with her husband Tom Goodyear, whose story appears on page 136.

MARGARET MIRIAM CROSS [RUSSELL]

DATE ENTERED SERVICE:
April 1943

DECORATIONS:
Canadian Volunteer Service Medal, Victory Medal

REGIMENT: RCAFWD

SERIAL #: W308200

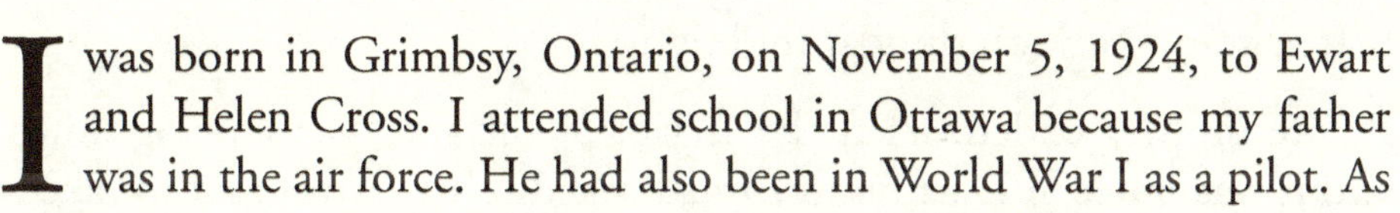

I was born in Grimbsy, Ontario, on November 5, 1924, to Ewart and Helen Cross. I attended school in Ottawa because my father was in the air force. He had also been in World War I as a pilot. As he was too old to be a pilot for the Second World War, he was in headquarters in Ottawa. At the age of eighteen, while I was in high school, I joined the RCAF Women's Division. My father had said to me when I joined, "Do not volunteer. Keep your eyes open and your mouth shut." Of course, I did not pay attention.

I did my training in Ottawa at Rockcliffe Air Force Base. From there I was sent to Halifax. While in Halifax, I worked at EAC, which was the Eastern Air Command in downtown Halifax and was situated near the Nova Scotian hotel. It was a big solid building, and our operations were conducted out of the basement. I was trained in fighter operations. I was one of the girls that you would see in an old movie, standing around a big table with a map on it. The map was sectioned into grids. The girls were there with their earphones on, with their long wands that had a magnet on the end. They would then pick up a little metal plane and put it on whichever grid they were told. A for Able, B for Baker, C for Charlie.

After Halifax I was sent to Sydney for a while and then Dartmouth. While in Dartmouth, the operations centre was off the base. A panel truck would pick a group of us up and drive us to the centre and bring us back after our shift was over. This truck had canvas over the top of it and a bench on each side to sit on. Our shifts were eight hours long, and there were three shifts a day. You would do about two weeks of the midnight shift, 12-8. I remember you would just be getting used to working at night and then you would be taken off and put on the day shift. I could never get used to the night shift.

When you are young, you can do foolish things. I remember coming off shift one morning and we went over to Halifax. This particular morning we went to give blood for which we received money. From there we went to a beach somewhere and enjoyed ourselves. Eventually, we headed back to barracks for a couple of hours sleep before going back on duty at midnight.

Before the war ended, I left the service as the war was slowing down and it was quiet in Dartmouth. I had asked to be transferred to take a course as a physical education instructor. Upon completion of this course, I would have the rank of sergeant. Unfortunately, the week before I was going to take the course, I fell on the ice and chipped my elbow and had to have it in a cast. This was the last course that was being offered for instructors. As a result, I asked for a discharge because I really felt I was not doing much.

By VE-Day I was out of the service and attending the Ryerson Institute in Toronto. I remember everybody just pouring out of the buildings. I knew a guy who had a motorcycle, and I got on back and we drove around the streets of Toronto. That fall I went to university. My husband-to-be, Fred Russell, whom I had met in Halifax before he went overseas, came to Toronto where I lived. We became engaged and that was the end of my university education. We were married the following June.

The war for me was not a terribly serious thing. I suppose I was helping the war effort. I thought I was doing my part, and you sort of live in your own area. I don't know if I had much knowledge about what was going on with the rest of the world. There used to be a slogan: "They also serve who only stand and wait." It is a good slogan because we did a lot of standing and waiting.

Looking back on it all now, the war helped change the lives of women. We worked at all sorts of occupations that we did not do prior to the war. When I was growing up, women had about three openings: a nurse, a teacher, or a secretary. When you got married, you were automatically finished at your job. This was the way that everybody saw it.

Peg Russell lives in Manuels. □□

This photo shows women placing planes on a metal grid, the type of work Peg Cross [Russell] did during the war.

CHAPTER 3

ROYAL NAVY

With the outbreak of hostilities in September 1939, the Royal Navy was short of trained crews. It was not long before a request went out for help from Newfoundland. Before the end of October, the Governor of Newfoundland, Sir Humphrey Walwyn, called for 625 volunteers for the Royal Navy. Less than a month later, the 1st Contingent, 200 men, left St. John's. They were the first troops from the British Commonwealth to arrive in England. The 1st Contingent was followed by 17 more, which also went overseas. In total, nearly 3500 Newfoundlanders joined the Royal Navy.

WILLIAM J.H. WINDSOR

DATE ENTERED SERVICE:
June 9, 1941

CAMPAIGNS:
Battle of the Atlantic

CONTINGENT: 16th

SERIAL #: JX299655

Bill Windsor was born about 1922, the son of Stanley and Mary Windsor. After his training, he did minesweeping duty around the coast of England. When he was returning home on his first leave, he was aboard the *Caribou*, which was sunk by a German U-boat on October 14, 1942.

Windsor was not one of the survivors. □□

The information about Bill Windsor comes from an interview with John Finn of St. John's, May 25, 2003.

NORMAN EDGAR FAREWELL

DATE ENTERED SERVICE:
August 28, 1941

CAMPAIGNS:
Malta Convoy, Invasion of North Africa, D-Day

DECORATIONS:
France and Germany Star, Africa Star 1942-1943, 1939-1945 Star, Newfoundland Volunteer Service Medal 1939-1945, Defence Medal, Victory Medal, The Atlantic Star with France and Germany Bar

SHIPS: HMS *Penn*, BYMS 2050

CONTINGENT: 17th

SERIAL #: C/JX315695

I was born in Creston, Placentia Bay, on September 7, 1923, to Tommy and Carrie Farewell. At the age of sixteen I went to work in the lumber woods and I left there to join the navy. When the war broke out, I was trying to join the army, but they told me I was not old enough.

I joined the navy in the summer of 1941, but we were in St. John's for quite a long while. After two or three months we left for England aboard the *Secharen*, which was an old German ship that was captured from the First World War. When we arrived in England, we were registered and were given our numbers. In our draft there were about 100 men. We were split up in two barracks, but the drafts were going so fast there were three drafts in the barracks at the same time. My training took place in Ganges, and I did not find the training hard because I had just come out of the lumber woods. Once you finished your training, you were given a week or so in London, and then you had to standby for the draft.

My first ship was the HMS *Penn*. We used to escort ships. We were sent into action really quick. First of all, we were given some training over in Norway, which was under German occupation at the time. We used to see our planes get hit, and they knew where we were in the event they were damaged in action. They were supposed to land alongside of us and we would go get them, but some thought they could make it across the channel [English Channel]. Not all of those made it.

My next action was in the Malta Convoy. This was the largest convoy of World War II. We had fourteen ships, filled with supplies to feed the people of Malta, in between 31 destroyers, cruisers, and aircraft carriers. Before we got very far, we lost one of our aircraft carriers, HMS *Eagle*. They tried to get some planes off her but they skidded down in the water. For five days and five nights we were at the gun trying to shoot down what was shooting at us. During this battle I was on a 4.7-inch gun, just like the one on the *Fort Amherst*.

As the action went on, they hit us really hard and split us up. Nine of the fourteen ships we were trying to protect were now gone. The next morning when we got up, we could see a ship on the horizon. We knew she was one of the convoy because she was drifting as she had been hit. It was the *Ohio* and it was right calm in the Mediterranean as we took her crew off.

We then expected the Italians to come in because we were right out in the middle of it. We figured they were going to get us. We then saw this mast sticking up over the horizon, and we watched and kept ourselves protected to make sure that we could see him just as quickly as he could see us. When he came over the horizon, we flashed him, and we realized it was the *Bramham*, which was another destroyer. We could not tow the *Ohio* because she would go the way her rudder was turned. It was decided that the *Penn* and *Bramham* would go on each side of the oil tanker. As the *Ohio* was lashed to the two destroyers, it took two days to get her precious cargo of fuel, which was essential to the island. The Germans used to come out and think it was a great shot, but what we used to do was have our destroyers on blake slips, and all you had to do was hit the blake and we would go on because we were a good target.

In the Malta Convoy, we had to deal with enemy aircraft and MTB's, which were motor torpedo boats. They would not come out and give you a good fight, but when the Germans came, it would be in three planes, and three behind them, and another three behind the front planes. They were trying to get us out of the way so they could get at the big ships. We went through hell getting that convoy in.

After the Malta Convoy I was involved in the invasion of North Africa. While in action we lost a lovely big cruiser, the *Manchester*. We tried to get the survivors off her, but somehow the Germans got them and brought them ashore to North Africa because the Vichy French were their Allies. I later found out that the British freed these POW's four months later.

I was involved in a few other minor skirmishes, and then I was assigned to a little minesweeper called BYMS 2050. On June 5, 1944, we left Portsmouth, England, in a wooden-hulled ship shortly after midnight to clear the way for the invasion. These ships had wooden hulls so they would not draw the magnetic mines. There were ten ships like ours in our section, and our mission was to clear the mines and drop these dan buoys in the water, and they had to be lit. We dropped our last dan buoy in thirteen feet of water and nobody fired on us. I will never understand that to this day. After we completed our mission, we had orders to turn south in the English Channel and go down the coast that way. The idea was to stay clear of the oncoming invasion fleet.

In our minesweeper there were nineteen of us, and there were seven of us from Newfoundland. One was Fred O'Brien, and he was a fine fella who came from Bell Island. We were not on the same watch but we were good friends aboard the ship.

About December 1944, I left my ship and came back to Newfoundland where I and my wife were married. They gave me three weeks leave and then I was going back to Chatham, England, to finish up my training in anti-aircraft gunnery courses. While here, the war ended in Europe, and what a celebration we had that night. They were climbing the fences and they started asking for people of every nation. When they asked for Newfoundland, I was the only one there so I had to go up.

While I was on my way to British Columbia to join the repair ship *Fifthnest*, they dropped the bomb on Japan to end the war. With the war over, we were supposed to leave the navy in drafts in order to get a discharge. But the Newfoundland government asked the Admiralty to discharge us as fast as they could, because once the Newfoundland winter set in, some places would be closed in. As a result many people would be stuck in St. John's and not get to see their families right away.

In February 1946 I received my discharge.

Norman Farewell passed away on January 18, 2006. □□

FREDERICK J. O'BRIEN

DATE ENTERED SERVICE:
July 30, 1940

CAMPAIGNS:
D-Day

DECORATIONS:
1939-45 Star, North Africa Star with bar, Atlantic Star, France and Germany Star, Defence Medal, Newfoundland Volunteer Service Medal

SHIPS: BYMS 2050

CONTINGENT: 10th

SERIAL #: JX216817

Fred O'Brien was born on Bell Island on April 12, 1918. He was on the minesweeper BYMS 2050, along with fellow Newfoundlander Norman Farewell, that helped clear the way for the invasion fleet headed toward the beaches of Normandy on June 6, 1944. On March 16, 1946, O'Brien was discharged.

O'Brien died on July 5, 2003, at the age of 86. □□

The information about Fred O'Brien comes from an interview with Norman Farewell, July 7, 2003.

JOHN MELVIN KING

DATE ENTERED SERVICE:
March 1, 1940

CAMPAIGNS:
Battle of the Atlantic,
Arctic Campaign

DECORATIONS:
1939-1945 Star, Atlantic Star, Pacific Star, The Defence Medal, The Newfoundland Volunteer Service Medal, Victory Medal, Russian Medal, Arctic Campaign Medal

SHIPS: HMS *Berwick*

SUBMARINES: H33, HMS *Dolphin*, P554, HMS *Volatile*

CONTINGENT: 11th

SERIAL #: PJX220879

I was born in Broad Cove, Conception Bay, on March 12, 1921, to William Josiah and Hannah Jane King. In 1939 it was a poor year for fishing, and in 1940 there was not much doing either.

I decided to join the navy, and while I was waiting to go overseas I was told that I could get a few weeks', or a few months' work. I went to the lumber woods up in the back of Curling [west coast of Newfoundland].

When we arrived they already had enough men, but because we had come from the east coast, they sent us to Cox's Cove, cutting wood and grinding pit-props. Eventually, two boats came in from England to take the pit-props. During this time I made 23 cents an hour, which was a lot of money then.

I went to England aboard the ship *Newfoundland* as part of the 11th Contingent, and there were about 190 of us in this draft. I was supposed to go over in the 5th, but my father became sick and I had to wait for a later draft. On the way over they were looking for volunteers to go in the submarine service. I volunteered along with Tommy Pitcher, Tommy Dower, Bob Sparkes, and Gerard McLennan. They are all dead now.

I did my training in Ganges, which did not last very long. I was drafted to the battle cruiser *Berwick*, where we saw some action with the German pocket battleship *Hipper*. That was Christmas Day 1940 when one of our turrets got hit and seven marines were killed.

When we came back to England for refitting, they caught me and said, "You volunteered for submarine service, didn't you?" I said, "Yes." Then they sent me for more training on the subs. This training was supposed to be six months long, but it was more like six weeks. I was drafted to H33, an old First World War training boat, which we did a couple of patrols in. In August 1942 I was drafted to HMS *Dolphin* for submarine service. While on the *Dolphin*, I was sent to Canada to help train the Canadian Navy. I was there for fourteen months. Then I was drafted to P554 for northern patrol. Sometimes we would see a U-boat from a distance, and if we went toward them they would dive and we would do the same thing.

When I returned from Canada, I was drafted to a brand-new submarine, HMS *Volatile*. We had our conning tower knocked off by one of our own destroyers. We were diving at the time that it happened but it was not deep enough. Then we went to Blighty, which is up off Newcastle, for repairs. When we returned, we had one more patrol and the war ended. I was then drafted to the first German sub to surrender during World

War II. U-1023 was on show all over England, Scotland, and Wales. One thing I noticed about the German subs was that they all had bunks to sleep in. All we had were hammocks, which I did not use because I always lay on two torpedoes. Their submarine was much the same as ours but everything was in German. We had a couple of German officers with us to help out. When I first joined the submarine service, I found the dives hard on my ears, but after, I got used to it. I was never sunk or torpedoed during the war. If I had my time back, I would do it all over again. On March 3, 1946, I was discharged with a rank of ABST [Able Seaman Torpedo Man].

Mel King lives in St. John's. □□

FRANK HERBERT LEWIS

DATE ENTERED SERVICE:
May 3, 1940

CAMPAIGNS:
Battle of the Atlantic, Arctic Campaign

DECORATIONS:
1939-45 Star, The Atlantic Star, The Africa Star, The Defence Medal, The Newfoundland Volunteer Service Medal, The Victory Medal, The National Commemorative Medal of Malta, The Russian Commemorative Medal 40th Anniversary, The Russian Commemorative Medal 50th Anniversary

SHIPS: HMS *Berwick*

CONTINGENT: 7th

SERIAL #: PJX200118

I was born on May 31, 1922, in St. John's, Newfoundland, to Frank and Carrie Lewis. When I was sixteen, I applied for the Royal Navy even though I had not finished school. In 1939 the HMS *Berwick* came to Newfoundland to escort the King and Queen over. At that time she was the flagship of the West Indies' Fleet. There were some people from Newfoundland who joined her here, but I was still too young. When the war started anybody that was patriotic joined, but there were a few who didn't. I joined the navy and my older brother Victor, who was one of the First Four Hundred in the artillery draft, joined the 59th. He was killed on manoeuvres about four or five months before D-Day. When I entered service, I was seventeen, but I turned eighteen on the way across aboard the RMS *Newfoundland*.

My training took place in Portsmouth, England. Herb Wells and I were in the same class. We did drill, gunnery, seamanship, and rigging. My training lasted about two and a half months and then we were all split up. In some cases five or six of us went to the one ship, and other times, one person would be sent to a ship themselves. In my case eight of us from Newfoundland went to the *Berwick*. The *Berwick* was a county class cruiser that had eight 8-inch guns and eight 4.7-inch guns, along with some smaller arms. She also carried two aircraft that used to catapult off her. When they returned to the ship, they used to land in the water alongside the ship, and a crane used to come out, hook on, and bring her in. One of our pilots was a fella named Rideout from Botwood, and we had a fella Power from Holyrood who used to pack the parachutes.

Our first battle was down in the Mediterranean with the Italian Fleet. The Royal Navy had three forces there and our force was stationed at Alexandria. On November 27, 1940, by 1:00 pm things were getting really hot. I had only been on the *Berwick* about three months, and out came this big Italian Fleet and we had quite a strong fleet also. We had a couple of aircraft carriers, which included the *Ark Royal*. We were in action for one hour. I was down in the magazine along with three others, passing up ammunition. We were the only ship in the whole fleet that got hit, with the loss of 14 men. We sank a couple of their ships and they made it back to their bases. After the naval battle, the Italians sent out their bombers and started to drop bombs on us. We were hit by Italian shells twice.

That evening, each body was put in a hammock, strapped up with rope, and their tags put on them. There were 14 of them on deck. There was the Roman Catholic padre and the Protestant padre. All the crew who could make it had to muster on quarterdeck. We had a trumpeter there with a plank on the guardrail. One body at a time was shot off. You could look back, see the wash, see the spray, and see the bodies. As we did, each ship in the fleet came in around our quarter.

Less than a month later, on December 25, 1940, we were escorting another convoy, once again screening her along with another cruiser. At dawn, wherever it was, it was foggy, misty, and cold. When you are at sea you automatically go to action stations in case there is something wrong. You stay there until daylight and then you go to breakfast. As a result of our previous action on November 27, my action station was taken out. It had killed every man on the turret. We were down under in the magazine. If the shell had elevated a little deeper, she would have gone up like the *Hood.* Instead of my usual action station I was up on the bridge on a place called the ADP. This was a direction finder, and there were about eight of us up there. We were the lookouts and we had chairs with binoculars attached. We didn't know anything and two big gun blasts went right across our bow. We got hit again, right through our oil tanks and into our flour, and what a god damn mess. One of the shells that hit us was a dud, because after a while, as the ship would roll, we would hear the shell roll. We lost two or three men that morning, and one was a Royal Marine. As we had a list on, we had to leave and get back to Gibraltar. The *Ark Royal* came out of Gibraltar and escorted us in. We stayed there for a while and then we went back to England because we were beat up after two actions. In the second battle we were hit by the German battleship *Hipper.*

When we returned to England for refitting, you would often get a leave while the ship was at dock. What usually happened was that one half of the ship's company went on leave for 21 days, and when they returned, the other half of the ship's crew would go on their leave. The Englishman would go home and the Newfoundlanders were given an amount of money to live on for 21 days. That would be gone within a week. What we used to do, and a good many of the byes did, was bring our coveralls on leave with us to London. When we ran out of money, we would go to work. A few of the guys went to work at Watley's Brewery. They would get a few pints of beer a day, a lunch, and at 4:30, you were paid. That was beer money for the night for us. Some other guys washed dishes at a hotel called the Savoy, which was behind the Caribou Club on Trafalgar Square.

After refitting we usually went up to Scapa Flow, which was up in the north of Scotland. From there we often ended up in the Denmark Strait where we spent a fair amount of time. There were two places there that we would go with another ship. There were the Val and Sadies fjords that were up between Greenland and Iceland. One ship would go in one of the fjords and put down anchor between two rocks or two hills. There was nothing up there but she could be there for two weeks. The other ship would go cruising up around the north of Iceland around the ice barrier. We were here because, if there were any German ships coming out, this is the way they would come. This was the way that the *Bismarck* came, and the *Norfolk* and the *Suffolk* were up there. They were the same class cruiser as the *Berwick.* We were up there with the *Cumberland* and we came down for a refit. This was where we were when the *Hood* got sunk. Sixteen Newfoundlanders went down with the *Hood*, including two Brewer brothers.

Next we went on the Murmansk run where we were shadowing convoys. We hardly ever saw the convoy as we were probably 40-50 miles off. The destroyers were in around the convoy itself. In November 1942 we escorted a convoy up and we had a mission to bring back an RAF wing. They had been there to show the Russians how to use the planes in order to fight the Germans. We brought them home for Christmas, but going up in November was hard weather, with the guns all iced up. Once you got up so far there was no daylight. I did two trips on the Murmansk run, actually two and a half because on one trip up we had engine problems and we couldn't keep up. We had to turn back and another cruiser took our place.

I was fortunate to have spent three and a half years on the *Berwick.* Some other people from Newfoundland who served on the *Berwick* were

Melvin King, Paul McDonald, who was a good buddy of mine, and Vince Wakeham, who received the DSM [Distinguished Service Medal] for his actions at Dunkirk. He and another guy went in an old drifter and made three or four trips to pick up British soldiers and evacuate them while under enemy fire. While on the *Berwick,* he was notified that he had to go to Buckingham Palace to receive his DSM.

Vince and I were the last two from Newfoundland to leave the *Berwick.* We went to Portsmouth where, after a period of time, I got a draft to go to the United States. The Royal Navy had a pool over in New Jersey. We had to go over there to pick up a new carrier, HMS *Reaper,* but she was not ready. It was going to be a month or so because she had to pick up her planes. We were in New Jersey a good while, and you could get a weekend pass and go up to New York. While I was there, I received some bad news about my brother. I was given leave to come home.

During my leave, VE-Day occurred. I got on the HMS *Highlander* in St. John's Harbour and returned to England. The war was over in Europe but there was still Japan. We still did not go to the Pacific, but we were waiting, waiting and more waiting. We were on leave up in London when we celebrated VJ-Day. London went up. I came back from leave and went to barracks at Portsmouth. I was then sent to Grennoch, a seaport in Scotland where they had a naval dockyard. The war was over and we were waiting to go home. While in Grennoch, they gave us money to stay in private boarding houses. We used to get up in the morning and work just like a civilian. We were dismantling destroyers. We were at that a while and then we got a draft to go back to barracks again. We came home in December 1945 aboard the *Queen Elizabeth.* On March 28, 1946, I received my discharge from the navy.

Frank Lewis passed away on September 9, 2003. □□

JAMES HUGH SHIELDS

DATE ENTERED SERVICE:
February 12, 1940

CAMPAIGNS:
Battle of the Atlantic, North Africa, Sicily, Italy, D-Day

DECORATIONS:
1939-1945 Star, Atlantic Star, Italy Star, Africa Star, Defence Medal, Newfoundland Volunteer Service Medal, Victory Medal

SHIPS: HMS *Derbyshire*, LST 367

CONTINGENT: 13th

SERIAL #: P/JX248015

I was born on October 26, 1920, in St. John's to James and Flora Shields. I grew up in the east end of LeMarchant Road where my father had a store. At the age of 12, I was in the Scouts, and at the age of 15, I was in the CLB [Church Lads Brigade]. In those days, I remember, everybody went to church, it was automatic. You went every morning, probably twice on Sunday.

When the war started, I wanted to get in it. I joined for a number of reasons. First of all, Great Britain was at war and in danger. In addition to that, we worked with the fellas who were in the First World War. It had only been twenty years since that time, and some of these men were only in their forties. We worked with them, and we figured if we could get enough Newfoundlanders over there, we could finish it up pretty quick, because we had no doubt of the ability of Newfoundlanders in a row. Another reason was that money was tight in those times, and if you wanted to see another part of the world, you had to get in something. Another reason was that you wanted to satisfy yourself that you could face action and conflict.

I joined the navy in February 1940. I was supposed to go over in the draft with Herb Wells, but I was injured while working at Lawlor's meat market, and I ended up in the hospital. It was a good while before I was called up. It turned out that there had been a mix-up and they thought I had gone over already. Finally, I went over with the 13th draft in November 1940, and it took 31 days to cross the Atlantic. It took so long because the old boat we were on, the *Baltrover*, had one engine break down and we did four knots all the way over on our own. On the way over we were lucky enough not to have any altercations with U-boats.

We arrived in England in December 1940, and we started our training shortly after. We trained in Ganges, which was near Ipswich, and I remember a lot of bombing going on. I did not mind the training, as a matter of fact, it was the fittest time of my life. Training lasted three months where we did things like navigation, knots, and taking boats out on the salt water. It was really thorough. I remember there used to be a mast in the middle of the parade ground that was 180 feet up. On the top of the mast there was a circular platform that was about three feet across which was called the button. There was always a Newfoundlander who went up there and would stand on top of it. I never did this because I was never one to overdo things, although I was not afraid of heights either, because I went up this height when I was on the ship.

After my three-month training course, I went to a training depot. This was where one of our draft was killed. On the parade ground there were bomb shelters if there was a bombing raid. This guy Ballam, a real nice guy, went in the shelter and a bomb dropped right on it. He never even got a chance to go out to sea. During the bombings I was part of the fire brigade because everybody was called in to do something.

After this, I was drafted to an armed merchant cruiser and I went right back across the Atlantic again. The AMC I was assigned to was the *Derbyshire* once I located her. She was in Halifax, but by the time we arrived, she had gone. I went aboard another AMC and went across the Atlantic again to Freetown, which was a main port for the convoys. We joined the *Derbyshire* and went convoying from Scotland down around the Cape of Good Hope and to the Mediterranean. Our ship was the only protection for the convoy, and we never had much to defend her with. We had a few old machine guns and a few depth charges. They were useless if it came to anything, but she was a lucky boat and a happy one. We had a great crew that had more than thirty Newfoundlanders aboard.

There were 25 of these armed merchant cruisers of which 15 were sunk. By 1942 they were decommissioned. After that, I went back to barracks, Portsmouth, where I did an anti-aircraft gunnery course. Upon completing this, I was drafted to the *Curacoa.* There were a half a dozen of us who were hung up in getting there, and she left before we arrived. They turned around and told us that the draft was cancelled, and as a result we returned to Portsmouth. I was then drafted to a landing craft, which was in the States as this was where they were being built. When I got up to Glasgow, we saw the *Queen Mary* and she had a big cut back on her bow. Then I heard the news that she had been in a collision with the HMS *Curacoa* and cut her in two. Once again I had been lucky.

We went to Boston aboard the *Queen Mary* and commissioned an LST, a landing ship tank, which was a big boat that was 3000 tons. In December 1942 we brought her to Halifax and then went home on leave. My leave lasted three weeks during which time I was married. My good fortune continued because I was married on December 12, 1942, which was the same night that the K of C [Knights of Columbus] hostel burned down with a great loss of life. If we had not decided to get married that night we would have been there.

After my leave I went back to New York to pick up another LST and we went out to the Mediterranean. We brought troops, tanks and other equipment to North Africa, Sicily, Salerno, and Anzio.

We moved troops in North Africa and we were involved in action there with German planes. I remember moving the Eighth British Army, some Americans, a Jewish regiment, but for the most part, it was the British Army. In 1944 we came back to England for D-Day. We brought our troops and supplies into Gold Beach on June 7, 1944. It was steady go. You did most of your loading in the nighttime, and once you were unloaded, you had to bring back the injured. There were a lot of damaged boats and stuff on the beach, and the LST's were not very manoeuvrable. As a result, you would get in one trip a day. We had little resistance because as far as we were concerned, we had total command of the air. All we had to do was worry about some of the things on the beaches. For us, delivering troops and tanks was routine to a great extent, as we had been doing this for a little under a year. A couple of weeks into the invasion I was injured. One of the stages broke loose, and I got a bit of a knock. It took all the skin off one of my legs. It was enough to have attention paid to it. I had to go back to the hospital in Portsmouth. When they started tangling around, they discovered something I always had. I had a scar on my lung and they figured I might have TB. I was in the hospital for a couple of months. They sent me home for a leave around September 1944. I then went to Avalon, which was a Canadian naval base in Buckmaster's Field. They had an anti-aircraft dome over on the South Side [St. John's]. This was where I taught until the end of the war, so on VE-Day, I was in St. John's, but I was wishing that I was over in England.

When it was all over, there was some adjustment, but my main concern was settling down and getting a job. I worked at the meat business, did a couple more things, and then opened my own meat market on Cookstown Road. When I look back on it all now, whatever doubts I might have had while serving, it is only when it was all over that you find out what went on and how lucky we were to beat them. When I read about it now, I have a great deal of satisfaction in what we did.

Jim Shields lives in St. John's. □□

ANGUS SAUNDERS PARDY

DATE ENTERED SERVICE:
March 22, 1941

CAMPAIGNS:
Battle of the Atlantic

DECORATIONS:
Distinguished Service Medal, 1939-45 Star, Africa Star, Burma Star, Italy Star, Newfoundland Volunteer Service Medal, Victory Medal

SHIPS: HMS *Farouk*, HMS *Birmingham*, HMS *Neaoli*, HMS *Essex*

CONTINGENT: 15th

SERIAL #: C/JX277316

I was born in Harbour Mille, Fortune Bay, on August 8, 1919, to William and Lenora Pardy. Before the war, at the age of fifteen, I was fishing on the Grand Banks. When Britain declared war on Germany, I did not feel very good about it. I decided to join, but I did not arrive in England until 1941.

We left St. John's aboard the HMS *Baltrover* and went to Halifax to join the convoy. On our passage over we ran into the U-boat pack, and I believe between eight and ten ships were sunk. Fortunately, our boat was not touched. We arrived in England and we did our training at a depot called Ganges. This lasted about six weeks. It was hard but I got through it. We covered every little thing you would need to know about the sea, even the compass.

After my training, I volunteered for secret service on HMS *Farouk*, which was a two-masted Egyptian schooner. We were out a little over a week when we ran into a hurricane. As a result the foremast was broke and we had to get towed to Egypt for repairs. We were in Egypt between three and four weeks. During this time we were sent into the desert to assist in driving Rommel [German field marshal] back from Alexandria. We were navy, but in this situation we were more or less soldiers. We all went in different directions, but the sub-lieutenant who was leading us was not very knowledgeable. We went in about 25 miles and the next thing we knew we walked right up alongside the Germans. They took us in for the night and we were prisoners of war. That evening, Rommel came and spoke to us and said, "You won't be here long. I'm expecting to be out of this tomorrow myself." I thought that Rommel was a really nice man.

My time in captivity was short and was not too bad. The next day, about 5:00 pm, the Germans were driven off by the British and they left us behind. In total I was a prisoner of war about 25 hours. After I was liberated, I went back to my ship *Farouk*. During our patrols we ran into two U-boats in a matter of a couple of weeks. We were fortunate to sink these. Our boat was well armed. [She had two guns hidden in a false deckhouse. The purpose was to lure U-boats to the surface.] It had a 3-pounder, a 5.5 and an Italian Lewis gun. The U-boats would come up alongside of us. We even had depth charges, but we did not have speed, which would later come back to haunt us.

On June 13, 1942, our luck ran out. On that day there was not a draft of wind, and as a result we could not sail. She did have a motor, but that was only used if the tide took us up on the rocks. We were twelve and a half miles off Turkey. When the torpedo hit, all hands went overboard, half of them frightened to death. [The HMS *Farouk* was sunk by U-83.] By the time I left the ship, the water was over my waist and I swam out of her. As I was swimming out, I noticed the old skipper was lying there breathing very heavy. He had a hole in his stomach and it looked as if his leg was broken. I lifted him up across a high post. I helped two or three other men from drowning. [Angus Pardy, along with another fellow Newfoundlander, Edgar Moss, received Distinguished Service Medals that day for their courage and determination in the Mediterranean.] We were fooling around then, trying to survive, me and the ASDEC [anti-sub detection] man. We decided to swim for shore. I swam eight and a half miles to the coast of Syria. When I was about a mile away from the coast, an Australian soldier came out to help me. When he came across me, he said, "Could I help you?" He would not come in alongside me, just in case I might grab a hold of him or something. I said, "Yes, sir, I am getting pretty weak." He then said, "I am coming underneath you." When he came in, I had been using my feet and hands, and I had been taking in water too before he came out. Without him I would not have made it ashore. When we got ashore, I could not stand on my own legs. In total I was in the water for more than eight hours.

By the time I arrived in hospital, the captain was already there with his leg up in a sling, laughing. The captain and the others stayed with the boat, and while I was swimming ashore, another boat came out to pick them up. Unfortunately, of the twenty-one on board, only five survived. I had to stay six weeks in hospital in Syria. The nurses taught me how to walk again as if I was only a small child. It was an enjoyable stay in hospital and there were plenty of nice nurses there. When I left the hospital, I joined the HMS *Neaoli* for patrol in African waters where we saw little action. From here I was drafted to HMS *Birmingham* for patrol in the Mediterranean. As she was a big cruiser, we were after submarines.

Sometime in 1943 I returned to England. I was then drafted to HMS *Essex* for patrol in the North Atlantic with St. John's as its port. I was home anyway. In June 1944 I was discharged from the navy.

Angus Pardy lives in Mount Pearl. □□

CHAPTER 4

Royal Air Force

In the spring of 1940, the Royal Air Force came to Newfoundland to recruit aircrew. More than 700 Newfoundlanders served with the RAF, either on the ground or in the air. Some men joined the Royal Canadian Air Force and either served in the RCAF or with various squadrons or elements of the RAF. The RAF Newfoundland Squadron, called the 125, was a night-fighter squadron given the task of defending Britain's coast against nocturnal attacks by enemy aircraft.

HOWARD KILPATRICK

DATE ENTERED SERVICE:
Unknown

CAMPAIGNS:
Northwest Europe, D-Day

DECORATIONS:
1939-45 Star, Aircrew Europe Star with France and Germany clasp, Canadian Volunteer Service Medal, Victory Medal

SQUADRON:
125 (Newfoundland) Squadron RAF

SERIAL #: R.C.A.F. J21639

I was born on February 15, 1921, in Whitbourne to Henry and Ella Kilpatrick. While growing up there, I worked at anything I could get a job at. I remember after school working at the fish markets and grocery stores. At the age of seventeen, I read Adolf Hitler's book, *Mein Kampf.* Here he was telling the world what he was planning, but nobody believed him. It was obvious, however, that someday, somebody was going to try and put a stop to what he was planning. This day came in September 1939 when Britain declared war on Germany after she invaded Poland. During this, I was a police officer with the Newfoundland Constabulary, which was my first steady job. With the war on, I wanted to be there, and in the air force. I chose the air force because I felt it was a nice clean way to live. My thinking was that you would have four or five bad hours at the most, and then you would return to a clean bed, dry sheets, and a heated room.

In the spring of 1940, the RAF arrived in Newfoundland to recruit aircrew. In the autumn of 1940, I was called up, but I was rejected for medical reasons. As I was determined to be part of the air force, I returned to work and saved enough money to go to Canada to join the RCAF. I had no trouble in getting in up there. After joining the RCAF in Halifax, I went to Lachine, Quebec, in a manning pool. Next I did tarmac duty, just being a Joe around the airport that was east of Montreal. From there I went to initial training school in Belleville, Ontario, and from there onto air observers' school in St. John's, Quebec. My next stop was the Y Depot in Halifax. For our passage to England we went down to New York to get aboard the *Queen Mary.* While in the UK I attended a radar school and finally went into an operational training unit where we went on operations.

In 1943 I was assigned to the 125 (Newfoundland) Squadron RAF, which was a night-fighter squadron. The task of our squadron was to patrol out to sea to intercept enemy aircraft. There were times when you had to scramble to intercept an unidentified plane, while other times you would be patrolling for four or five hours over the continent. At times, on these patrols we mixed it up with JU 88s. The first type of plane that I was a navigator and radar operator on was the Beaufighter Mark V1. These were quite good airplanes for their day, but were not quite as good as the Mosquitoes that we ended up with.

I had three crashes during the war, but the biggest occurred on December 28, 1943, while we were in a Mark V1 Beaufighter. We were scrambled that night for an unidentified aircraft that was coming in. By the time we got in position, the plane had been identified. While we were in the air, we said, we were going to stay up and do a few hours practice. When we got into position, our starboard engine quit. We headed toward the nearest station which was only about 50 miles away. When the starboard engine failed we did not have any hydraulics system. My job was to stand behind the pilot and pump down the wheels by hand as we approached the aerodrome. While I was doing this, the other engine failed, and I knew then that we would not require wheels. I got up and jettisoned my parachute by turning a button on the harness, and that fell off. Next I took off my helmet as it was wired onto the end of the communications system. Then I jettisoned the escape hatch in the roof of the airplane, and that was all there was to it. We crashed a mile and a half from the end of the runway at a speed of about 120 mph. The airplane was completely destroyed, which is quite common in aircraft crashes, but mainly because of fire. Our aircraft never caught on fire; it just smashed to pieces. There was nothing salvageable.

Even though there was a war on we had more good times than bad. We were even fortunate enough that Mr. Churchill decided that operational aircrews could have a gasoline ration. I had a motor car over there, driving around the countryside. On my second or third leave, I met a girl whom I eventually married in 1944. She lived in London during the blitz. I remember the roof was blown off her house on two separate occasions by buzz bombs. Germany made very little effort against Britain in the air as the war went on. They tried to blitz the civilian population but that did not work. They also tried buzz bombs and V2s. The Germans also made hit-and-run operations on England, which nobody really cared about at all. They came in with these Foch-Wulf 190s, which were good fighter planes, armed with 200-kg bombs. They crossed the channel, just skimming the water, and once they reached the coast, they would climb between eight and ten thousand feet. When they thought they were over London, they jettisoned the bomb because they could not aim it. They would then turn and go back to Germany. We did not know it at the time but they only had twelve planes for this, and undoubtedly they would lose one now and again. We were always under the impression that they could launch another attack.

We started over the continent before D-Day. I remember we spent a lot of time over Holland trying to find the launching sites of the V2s. Just after midnight on the morning of June 6, 1944, we were on patrol for a couple of hours right over the beachhead. There was nothing happening at the time because the shooting did not start until daylight. We carried on normal patrols, nothing extra so as not to bring any added attention to the invasion area. The next night when we went over again, there was obvious action on the ground, but we never encountered any resistance. The Germans did, however, send a few planes out over the next days, but that soon came to an end. They did have aircraft but they were being used on the Russian front.

On May 7, 1945, Mr. Churchill announced that the next day would be Victory in Europe Day. As a result, everything would be stood down with the exceptions of two aircraft in every night-fighter squadron. Those who volunteered would get a 48-hour pass. In our squadron, our flight commander and his navigator were one plane, and I saw to it that my pilot and I were the other. I wanted to see my wife in London, and by coincidence my pilot was also from London.

We were the two crews on immediate readiness that night, while everybody else was out celebrating all over the aerodrome. At dusk, there were seven of us, four aircrew, a mechanic crew chief to start us up if necessary, and two girls, one a lorry driver and the other a clerk, all sitting down talking and talking. Finally, a little after 1:00 am, after reviewing the entire war, the navigator, named Bill, said, "You know, chaps, you realize we now stand a good chance of dying in bed." That was a very profound thought. We always knew we were employed in a high-risk occupation, but I hadn't looked that far ahead. I guess that was the general feeling all over. I was discharged at Torbay, station # 1 sub release. When I look back on it all now, the comradeship is something that cannot be described, my God, if we only lived together like we fought together, yes indeed, wonderful.

Howard Kilpatrick passed away on January 24, 2006, in St. John's. □□

SOLOMON AUGUSTUS BUTT

DATE ENTERED SERVICE:
Unknown

CAMPAIGNS:
Unknown

SERIAL #: **NFU** 1689

SERIAL #: **RAF** 1371681

Gus Butt was born on September 2, 1918, on Flat Island, Bonavista Bay, son of Solomon Butt and Fedora Randell. His father passed away when he was a baby and his mother moved back to Port Rexton. When she passed away, he was raised by his uncle Charles Bannister Randell and his wife Elizabeth. Before the war broke out, he fished on the Labrador for two summers. One summer he was aboard the schooner *Governor Anderson*, and another he was aboard the schooner *Evelyn L. Crosbie*. He also worked in the lumber woods in Indian Bay.

With the outbreak of the war, Butt joined the Newfoundland Overseas Forestry Unit, where he did his required six months service. He then transferred to the Royal Air Force. One of the places he was stationed was a base up in the Shetland Islands. His rank was Leading Aircraftman and he was an airplane mechanic. While in Scotland, Butt met and married his wife Elizabeth Sharpe, and they had two children.

Gus Butt passed away in Toronto on January 7, 1995. □□

The information about Gus Butt comes from an interview with his cousin Ralph Randell, August 2003.

JAMES JOSEPH FINN

DATE ENTERED SERVICE: Unknown

DECORATIONS: ER Commemorative

SQUADRON: 125 (Newfoundland) Squadron

SERIAL #: 798668

James Finn was born in St. John's to Mike and Catherine Finn. He flew Mosquitos for the RAF. "On January 15, 1943, Flight Sergeant Finn, who had only recently joined the squadron, was lost at sea when forced by engine trouble to bale out with his navigator."* Another story has it that he was shot down over the English Channel. In either case his body was never found. □□

The information about James Finn comes from G.W.L. Nicholson, *More Fighting Newfoundlanders*, and from an interview with his brother John Finn of St. John's, May 18, 2003.

* Nicholson, G.W.L. *More Fighting Newfoundlanders*, page 416.

CHAPTER 5

□□

Royal Artillery

In the *Newfoundland Gazette* of February 6, 1940, there was an article asking for volunteers for a heavy regiment of the Royal Artillery to serve with the British Army. By April 1940, the First Four Hundred left St. John's. Initially, the Newfoundland volunteers were the 57th Newfoundland Heavy Artillery. With further drafts arriving, these groups were split into two regiments, the 166th and the 59th. The 166th was a field regiment that fought in North Africa and Italy. Of all the British units, the 166th was in continuous action the longest. The 59th helped to defend the coast of Britain from possible invasion, and in July 1944, landed in France and made its way through northwest Europe.

ERIC THOMSON BAGGS

DATE ENTERED SERVICE:
March 27, 1940

CAMPAIGNS:
North Africa, Italy

DECORATIONS:
Military Medal, 1939-45 Star, Africa Star, Italy Star, Newfoundland Volunteer Service Medal, War Medal, Victory Medal

REGIMENT:
166th (Newfoundland) Field Regiment R.A.

DRAFT: 1st

SERIAL #: 970041

I was born in St. John's on March 3, 1918, to Joseph Baggs and Margaret Halliday Thomson. I grew up in the west end on Leslie Street and attended school at Prince of Wales College. In 1933 I graduated from grade 11 and went to work at the Royal stores. In 1937 I was accepted for the RAF but my father would not let me go as I was underage.

Shortly after the outbreak of the Second World War, the Royal Artillery were looking for volunteers. At the age of 21, I was one of the first 50 to join on the first day. I joined more for the adventure than anything, and to get out of the routine. After joining in March, we used to fall in at the CLB [Church Lads Brigade] Armoury. That year we had no snow and we did not have any pavement in those days except the cobblestones on Water Street. I remember marching up Freshwater Road and back to the armoury. Basically, we were trying to get in some shape.

On April 14 we left Newfoundland. We encountered no resistance on the way over and we landed in Liverpool. Next we boarded railway cars, which were like our old second-class cars. They took us across England to Woolwich. At Woolwich, we marched up to the Grand Depot of the Royal Artillery. The next morning we were paraded to the quartermaster's stores and issued uniforms. Most of them were either too large or too small.

Next we all had personal interviews in order to assess what we would be best suited for. Some went to signals school while others to drivers' school. Of the 404 who came over, there were only two of us left on the parade ground, Ted Tooton and I. We wanted to be mechanics. Teddy was a mechanic while I was an amateur one. We were sent to a place called Sussex, and when we arrived, there were five motor vehicles not operating. After getting the first one operational, there was no problem getting the others going.

I also made a mistake. I repaired the sergeant major's motorcycle and took it for a test run. I did not think anything more of it until after Dunkirk. During this time we were waiting for an invasion from Hitler's troops. As a result, wireless silence was enforced. You could not send a message back and forth. Because of this, they needed dispatch riders. Sergeant Major Erquart knew I had repaired his motorcycle and taken it for a test run. He ordered me away from my job as duty driver for the commanding officer and to drive his motorcycle to RHQ [regimental headquarters] in Norwich which was about 40 miles away.

As a dispatch rider I rode for ten days and ten nights without going to bed. Eventually, I crashed my bike into a hawthorn hedge and went ass over kettle into a field. Other than scratches, I did not get hurt. After this incident I turned in my gear and told the captain I was not driving anymore. The sergeant major said, "You are refusing to obey an order." I said, "No, sir, I refuse to get killed stupidly." He permitted me to go to bed and I slept for two days solid. Next they wanted me to go to military college in North Wales but I declined. I joined the army to be a soldier and I wanted to be on the guns. They put me on the guns and I never looked back.

I was in Roger Battery, F Troop. I had a first-class gun crew and I was a very good sergeant. We were finished our training in Scotland where we had our last firing camp at Northumberland Moors. By the time we boarded the *Circassia* to leave, we were well trained. We went across the Irish Sea through rough weather, and most of our lads became sick. We landed on floating jetties in Algiers, but we did not go ashore. We were then taken on two ships, the *Queen Emma* and *Princess Beatrix*, up the coast about 300 hundred miles to a place called Bone. From here we marched in about five miles to a staging area. We were there several weeks until our guns arrived. They came out in a slow convoy.

The Kasserine Pass was when we came under shellfire for the first time. Jimmy Winter was killed and Frank Simms was wounded. After this we moved to various positions as we pushed the enemy back. At Medjez-el-Bab we supported the Argyle and Sutherland Highlanders. They took Longstop Hill. After that we swung south. I remember my buddy Ted Tooton, who was staff sergeant. He used to ride up to my gun every day we were in Africa and talk about our plans after the war. I asked Ted if he had any plans. He said, "I am going to leave my black bones here in Africa." God damn it, he got killed that morning. There were a bunch of camels there that were heavily shelled, and Ted got the top of his head blown off. This hit me hard as we were as close as fleas.

At a place called Zaghouan I was awarded the Military Medal. This was the final round-up in Tunis and the Cape Bon Peninsula. On an airfield, the troop I was in, Freddie Troop, and I was the number one gun. There were only individual targets and our captain, who was up in a windmill trying to spot what was what. However, he did not see that they were firing across the airfield at us over open sights. I was getting short on ammunition and I called out to George Downtown who was acting sergeant major. I said, "Downtown, get me a load of ammunition." As he unloaded the ammo, he turned to me and said, "Baggs, give me a cigarette." I said, "That is the last fucking cigarette I will ever give you." He did not live five minutes afterwards. The top of his head was blown off. Ralph Kelloway and Dick Dormody also died. I was wounded also, as I was hit in the back of the head, but I got my gun back. We got spare tires from each of the other gun crews and got her back in action. By this time I had lost so much blood I was not able to do any lifting. I said, "Jack her up, boys, and change the wheels." The late Leo Stamp was the one they gave me from Pius Jesso's gun. Stamp said, "Jack her up be god-damned, Sarge. You tell the guys to slack up the lugs and I will lift her up." A 25-pounder weighs a ton and three quarters. When the lugs were loose on one side, Leo went around and with a back lift, tipped the gun up. They changed the wheel and then he went over to the other side.

After we left Africa, we went to Italy. Our first action was on the Sangro River. I was over with the observation party, and all the sergeant majors went over to pick out spots for their troop. I was the sergeant major of Don Troop. We had crossed the Sangro on a pontoon infantry bridge, but one of our own fighter aircraft bombed it and blew it up. Here we were, stranded, and we were supporting the 4th Indian Division at the time. Col. Hitchcock was asking everyone in turn if they thought they could get back. They said they could not ride well enough. I was the junior sergeant and when he asked me, I said, "Yes, sir, I can get back." When I got down to the Sangro, there was a bridge with a plank about a foot wide, and it was a fairly good-sized river. The infantry had made a little footbridge for running across. I looked at it and said, "Jesus, I'll never make that." In the meantime I put the bike in gear, got her going and went across.

I remember we were very lucky at Cassino the day of the big assault. The Yanks came in with 85 bombers every 15 minutes. A large proportion of these bombers dropped their bombs behind us and they knocked out a couple of English field artillery regiments and one medium regiment. I used to stand with the tanoy, what we called the loudspeaker. As soon as I'd see the bomb bays open, I'd tell the boys to stand by. When the bomb bays opened, and I judged the bombs to be coming this way, I'd say, "Take cover," and everybody would dive down in the trenches. While at Cassino we were at long-range machine-gun fire.

After Rome fell, our guns all went back to ordnance to get new barrels put in and to be recalibrated and so on. The guys then were permitted at different times to go on leave and go around Rome.

We were 185 days on the front lines, the longest any troops have been on the front lines. An infantry division is in anywhere from 15-18 days and they are taken out for a rest. We belonged to what they called corps troops, and we were just left there, and when the new division came in or if another division needed more firepower, we could be called to assist them. We were back and forth from the Adriatic to the Tyrrhenian side of Italy. It is only 125 miles across Italy, but you have to go over the mountain ridge through the snow, and that was one hell of a move. We never encountered any resistance during these moves as there was always infantry in front of us.

We were considered to be part of the D-Day Dodgers. We only laughed at this. The second front would not have been possible had it not been for Kesselring [German field marshall] committing his best paratroopers to the north of Italy. They thought we were going to go through the soft belly of Italy. There were quite a few German divisions tied up in Italy.

I was discharged on February 21, 1946. On my discharge certificate it stated: "His ability, energy, and devotion to duty during his military service gained for him the rank of Warrant Officer Class and recommendation for promotion to commissioned rank." That is as good as it gets. If I had to do it all over again, I would.

Eric Baggs resides in St. John's. □□

RONALD E.J. WHITE

DATE ENTERED SERVICE:
March 28, 1940

CAMPAIGNS:
North Africa, Italy

REGIMENT:
166th (Newfoundland) Field Regiment R.A. (137 Battery)

DRAFT: 1st

SERIAL #: 970054

Ronald White was born on July 13, 1919, to Walter and Edith White and grew up on Leslie Street in St. John's. He was part of the First Four Hundred. While in England, the 57th, which later became known as the 166th, did extensive training protecting England's west coast from a possible invasion from the enemy. The 166th saw their first action in North Africa. On November 29, 1943, White was killed in action near a small town called Mozzagrogna. As the story goes, he was walking a donkey and it stepped on a land-mine, killing them both. □□

The information about Ronald White comes from Harold Lake, *Perhaps They Left Us Up There*, page 114, and from an interview with Art White of St. John's, May 2003. Art White is the younger brother of Ron White, and the story of the land-mine was told to him by a member of the 166th in the Corner Brook area.

WILLIAM MINTY MORRY

DATE ENTERED SERVICE:
April 1, 1940

CAMPAIGNS:
North Africa, Italy

DECORATIONS:
Service Star 1939-1945, Newfoundland Volunteer Service Medal, Africa Star, Italy Star, Defence Medal, Victory Medal, Canadian Centennial Medal, Queen's Jubilee 25-year Medal, Canadian Decoration, Queen's Jubilee 50-year Medal

REGIMENT: 166th (Newfoundland) Field Regiment R.A.

DRAFT: 1st

SERIAL #: 970271

I was born in Ferryland, Newfoundland, on February 21, 1918, to Howard and Fredris Morry. My middle name was Minty, which was my mother's name. She was a war bride and came from Scotland as my father served in the First World War. Before the war I did some fishing, but I worked on the land mainly. I then joined the police force, which I was in three years before I joined the army. I remember hearing Hitler when he started to rant and rave. He used to send chills up my back. When the war broke out, my brother Reginald had already gone in the navy. I never had a feeling for the sea at all. I said right from the start I was going, but I was waiting for the army to start recruiting. This is why I was part of the First Four Hundred.

One reason I joined the army was because it was in my background. My father and my two uncles were in the First World War. Some of the places my father served were Gallipoli and Beaumont Hamel. My grandfather was a member of the British Army that captured Louis Riel. I also had an uncle who went in the forestry unit in the Second World War as he was too old to get in anything else. In addition, I felt a duty to go. Some people say we went for the adventure, but I don't think that really came in, not with me, nor with a lot of the others. We certainly didn't go for the pay. If you were working at all, you were getting five or six times the pay that you were getting in the army. Our pay was two schillings a day, 48 cents a day. Even though I was interested in joining, my father was always telling me not to go. He said, "Your brother is gone and you shouldn't go." When I enlisted, I didn't say a word, but I did call him and tell him.

We left St. John's on April 14, 1940, and landed in Liverpool on April 25. We started our training, but it was not like you would get in peacetime, because there was a war on. We did marching, route marches, but I would say that the training was what the circumstances permitted. It wasn't steady training, but you did get used to the basics of training, wearing your boots, your uniform, anti-gas training, small arms training, and things like that. Another part of our training was the coastal defence of Norwich and Norfolk.

Before long, as a result of my initial training on the police force I received a stripe. A short while after, I received two more and was promoted to sergeant. Some of us who had left the police force were even given men to put them through their basic training. We had no idea how to train people so we were not very successful. At first we were the 57th and I was part of A Battery, and then we formed the 166th and I was in Q Battery or Queenie as it was called for a while. Then I was promoted to P Battery where I spent the rest of the war. When we became the 166th, we became a field regiment which was a completely different thing altogether. We went to Salisbury Plain and this is where we took our training. We were put on the 25-pounders because the colonel felt that as long as we were on the heavies, we would just be on coastal defence in England. He was a veteran of the first war and he wanted to get in on the action. This is why we went into the field artillery.

Our first stop was in North Africa. The action here was more like a naval war between ships. For the most part there were very few hills or mountains, only sand hills. As a result tanks played a major role as they could come from any direction. We landed up in a little town called Setif, which was in Tunisia where there were some hills.

The first casualty that we had, or that I was aware of, was a fella Flynn. We were in the hills and he did what he was supposed to do when we were receiving enemy shells. He jumped into his slit trench, and the shell went right in with him. It was not very often that this happened. We were there in those hills in Tunisia for a while and then we were moved farther south down toward Tunis where we were on the sand. While in North Africa, we had quite a few casualties. Had our rate of casualties been the same for the full time as we had in North Africa, we would have had very high casualties because of the circumstances. We had several men killed on mines and other forms of action. The weather was terrible there, because it wasn't fit to live in during the day, as it was so hot, and during the night we froze to death. The fluctuation in the weather between day and night was unbelievable.

While in North Africa, we fought against the Germans and Italians. The Germans were very good soldiers and had a very good general. Rommel [German field marshal] was so popular with us that the powers-that-be were a little leery of it. He was such a fair man, a great general, and he was on the front lines. He believed in the Geneva Conventions. He did not allow anything to be done to the prisoners. Once you were taken a prisoner, you were treated as a prisoner of war.

The Italians, on the other hand, were not very good soldiers and were happy-go-lucky types. For instance, when we took prisoners, the Italians would line up for food with us, whereas with the German prisoners, they had to be always under guards armed with machine guns or they would run away.

When [General] Montgomery came along, he was very popular with us also. He did not get along well with his equals because of the kind of person he was, but he got along extremely well with the men in the lower ranks.

I remember being in a slit trench with Bern Lannon of Grand Falls, and we were having a chat while under shellfire. It was not heavy but we were right open from Longstop Hill in view of the Germans. They were popping at us and we were popping at them. We were keeping our heads down but I heard Bern say, "Look at the man in the air." I heard him say this but I don't know who else did. When I looked up, he was sitting there with his face all bashed in. He looked up just as a big cloud of earth came down and hit him in the face and killed him. A little while after, they came around looking for the gun mechanic because a gun had been damaged. Nobody had seen him but I thought about what Bern had said. I told them what Sergeant Lannon had told me and they found him. He was an Englishman who was killed, and there was not a mark on him. He was blown up in the air by a shell and a concussion had killed him. Bern had seen him going up in the air.

Overall, the campaign in North Africa was a tough one. There were no lines or strong points. This is why the Germans were on top for so long, they had an extremely good general and they were more mobile than we were. They had better tanks in the beginning, much better. They had better training and were better equipped, generally speaking. Then the Americans started to arm us, we got General Grant tanks, which were much better than the Matilda or Waltzing Matildas as we called them. The Matilda had thin armour and very small guns. Finally we had better equipment, more manpower, and better lines of supply. That is why we eventually beat the Germans in North Africa. It was supply more than anything.

After North Africa, we landed in Sicily but we did not take part in any action because there was no room. We made our way down to Taranto in southern Italy in the heel of the boot and came up that way. In Italy there was a lot of slogging, heavy work, going up mountains and crossing rivers. During fighting in Cassino, my second-in-command, Reg Freeman, who came from Norris Arm, was killed right beside me. I will never forget that.

I had a couple of injuries during the war. I had a wood splinter from a shell. I did not even know it happened until one of the men told me. I lifted up my arm and it was bleeding. I went back, had it sewn up, and I had to go around in a sling for a while. I did not lose any time. Another time I dropped a box of 25-pounder ammunition on my right foot and crushed it. It gives me a little trouble today, but not much.

When D-Day was on, we were still fighting in Italy. I remember Lady Astor referring to us as the D-Day Dodgers. She came out on the platform and talked about the scruffy lot, our boys in Italy, an untidy dirty looking bunch, not like our nice clean boys that went over on D-Day. We had more than two years of active service and action in bad weather and circumstances you would not wish on a dog. It did not go over very well and there was also a song made up about it.

We were in action a long time, and we didn't recognize this syndrome that they talk about today. We had fellas that came back and became drunks, and some others went in the mental asylum and never got out again. They cracked up mentally under the strain. Others, their stomachs gave out like mine, but that was something you could live with. When you came out, unless you lost a leg or something, they gave you a Grade A discharge. Later on, you found out you had problems, you had to go before a medical board.

In February 1946 I was discharged and on my discharge certificate it said: "Military Conduct Exemplary." This was the highest you could get. After that I went back in the police force for a couple of years, and then I went back to Ferryland and took over the family business.

Bill Morry passed away in St. John's on October 11, 2004. □□

HOWARD ARCHIBALD BUTLER

DATE ENTERED SERVICE:
March 20, 1940

CAMPAIGNS:
North Africa, Italy

DECORATIONS:
Service Star 1939-1945, Newfoundland Volunteer Service Medal, Africa Star, Italy Star, Defence Medal, Victory Medal

REGIMENT: 166th (Newfoundland) Field Regiment Royal Artillery

DRAFT: 1st

SERIAL #: 970223

I was born on Brazil Square in St. John's on May 15, 1918, to Jim and Beatrice Butler. I grew up on Sulva Street and attended the Parade Street school which was more commonly known as the "Tabernacle." This was located on the former site of Dominion supermarket, where the new fire department is being built today. From there I went to Prince of Wales on LeMarchant Road, which is now condominiums.

When Britain declared war on Germany in September 1939, I thought it was only right, but was Britain ready? Germany had already taken the Rhineland, Austria, Czechoslovakia, and when she attempted Poland,

Britain declared war. I joined the army because I thought it was my duty. The empire was at war and I was a loyal subject of the empire. I preferred the army because I was a landlubber and I had no experience at sea. I became part of the First Four Hundred to join the Royal Artillery.

In April 1940 we left Newfoundland and eventually boarded the *Duchess of Richmond*. This was a luxury liner and we traveled like first-class passengers. We had a pleasant trip over without seeing any U-boats. When we arrived in England there was a lot of panic all over because of the possibility of the Jerries [Germans] invading. We had a strong navy but other than that we didn't have much to fight with. I remember there were plenty of invasion scares where we turned out to face the possible invaders, but they never came.

Our first year of training we were the 57th Heavy Gun Regiment, and we trained on 6-inch guns while some other batteries had 9.2's, which were all World War I weapons. In November 1941 we became the 166th Field Regiment, which made us more mobile. We did training exercises in different parts of England, like Wales, West Moorlands, and Salisbury Plain. Besides training on the guns, we did marching and spit-and-polish parades. I remember being inspected by General Paget, who was the commander-in-chief of the Home Forces at Larkhill, Salisbury Plain.

In January 1943 we boarded the *Circassia*, which was bound for North Africa. This was not like our voyage on the *Duchess of Richmond*. Instead of comfortable living quarters, we slept in hammocks. In addition, we went through some rough seas as the *Circassia* rolled and pitched, rolled and pitched. Practically the entire regiment was seasick. After landing we were some weeks in a transit camp before our equipment arrived in a separate ship. During our waiting period we used to go on fatigues. We were a labour force at the base supply depot. When our equipment arrived, we started to move inland. First of all we were in a gun position supporting the French. Next we moved to the First Army Front to take part in the barrage against Longstop Hill, which was a German bastion barring the road to Tunis. There were something like 300 guns opened up against Longstop. I remember being there in a slit trench with two others, and we were being shelled.

They say you won't hear the one that hits you, but this one was very slow. It was dropping right down on us, and when it burst it scattered gravel and pebbles on top of us. None of us were touched, but it was a scary time. The Germans held out for a day and a half before they retreated.

We then did further training in Setif during September 1943. In October we landed by landing craft in Italy. Once we got organized we met up with Montgomery's Eighth Army. After some fierce fighting we took the Sangro. In Italy there were a lot of mountains, which led to difficulty in getting around. We supported the Canadians in Ortona, which eventually fell. While in Italy, we faced the 21st Panzer Division and paratroopers of the Hermann Goering Division. During these campaigns I was a signaller with Pip Battery. My job was to pass fire orders on and to receive messages. As signallers, we worked with wireless sets, field telephones, and ten-line exchange. There was always a signaller on the job and we had to be accurate.

Our next objective was Rome, but during the winter of 1944 we were stuck in the Apennines Mountains, and the Germans were below us. We exchanged fire sporadically. With the second front coming soon, Monty was taken back to England to lead the British. With his departure, we lost our inspired leader and we did not make the same advances.

I arrived home on May 8, 1945, which was the same day the war ended in Europe. I believe the Germans in Italy surrendered a few days before. We were supposed to go back but the Japanese surrendered shortly after too. I was discharged on September 16, 1945. When I got home I felt like a fish out of water. It's a funny thing, you know, when I was in the army I swore on it, but I missed it when it was gone. I met my wife-to-be on June 11, 1945, and we were married in March of the next year. We had four children, one of which joined the Canadian armed forces. After spending all that time together, there is definitely a bond between us. My wife and I attended several reunions over the years and enjoyed them thoroughly. If I had to, I would do it all over again.

Howard Butler died on October 14, 2004. □□

ERIC JOSEPH HAMMOND

DATE ENTERED SERVICE:
Newfoundland Militia,
Nov. 11, 1942
R.A., July 8, 1943

CAMPAIGNS: Italy

DECORATIONS:
1939-45 Star, Italian Star, Newfoundland Volunteer Medal, 1939-45 War Medal, Defence Medal

REGIMENT:
Newfoundland Militia, 166th (Newfoundland) Field Regiment R.A.

SERIAL #: 1054, 971918

I was born in St. John's on November 23, 1923, to John and Elizabeth Hammond. I started school at St. George's on Merrymeeting Road, which is now the Hub. From there I did grades 6-9 at Springdale Street, and I completed grade 10 at Bishop Feild College.

When the war started in 1939, I was sixteen and attending school. Upon completion of school, I went to work at Bowring Brothers on Water Street. At the age of 18, my friend and I tried to enlist in the RAF but they were not accepting anybody at this time. I continued to work at Bowring's until I joined the Newfoundland Militia on November 11, 1942. In order to have the opportunity to go overseas, you had to have some initial training. The only way to get this training was through the militia. We did rifle drill and marching, which was helping to prepare us for overseas duty. Some of our duties included security duty on the naval dockyard in St. John's. I also did guard duty on Bell Island, Bay Roberts, and Harbour Grace.

On July 8, 1943, I enlisted in the Royal Artillery. They needed some replacements and they would often take about 50 at a time in a draft. I went over in a draft but I cannot remember the number. We went over on the *Queen Elizabeth* without any convoy. She was so fast that she would have been a sitting duck in a slow convoy. Rumour had it, there were 23,000 soldiers on board. We did not encounter any U-boats along the way, and we arrived in Grennoch, Scotland. We were ferried to the wharf, and then we boarded a train to a place called Watford, which was just outside London. While there, we lived in tents in a beautiful park. Next we did some tests and we were sorted out for different things. I was picked with three others for a specialist course which took place in Newtown, central Wales. By the time we arrived, the course had already started three weeks before. This meant we did our training, and we had to catch up in the evening. This was followed by initial training on the 25-pounders. After this we went to the east coast of England to a place called Alford in Lincolnshire to continue training. From there to Cromer, Norfolk, for training on medium and heavy artillery like 4.5s, 5.5s, and also 7.2s. By this time, we were well trained.

In order to assist in placing members of the Royal Artillery, the Newfoundland government set up a depot. This was a transit station, which was a few miles up the coast to Shearingham. I was one of the first people to go through this depot. We were there for a couple of months and while there I was assigned to the 166th. As a result we were shipped off to Italy. We landed in Naples on October 7, 1944. We stayed at Eboli for a few months. We had to wait for orders to move as a regiment can only take so many people at a time. Eventually, I believe, there were six of us who went to another transit station in central Italy.

Finally, on December 9, 1944, we went to join the 166th, which was at this time north of Florence, where they were dug in, up in the mountains. As a replacement everything went fine, and I fit in well. I had a fairly good record which obviously followed me. The second day there I was told to go on the gun as layer, which I knew was a test. The next day I was made the gun layer. This is the person who sets the range, elevation, angles, and so forth, as passed down from the forward observation party, on the sights and fires the gun.

As I came to the regiment late, I was not involved in battles such as Cassino, Liri Valley, or Sangro River. The only action that I was involved in was in the north of Florence when they were dug in. During this time there were some exchanges of sporadic gunfire. I do remember the Germans dropping propaganda leaflets on us.

On February 18, 1945, the 24th Guards Brigade, which the 166th were supporting, were being withdrawn. As a result the 166th, which was long overdue for a rest, also was relieved. The war was winding down in Italy, and I received a layer's pay, which was unknown in wartime. I was also promoted to lance bombardier. I received my discharge on November 5, 1945, and once home I went back to work at Bowring Brothers, where I worked 52 years in total.

Eric Hammond lives in St. John's. □□

JOHN PATRICK JOSEPH MARCH

DATE ENTERED SERVICE:
August 7, 1940

CAMPAIGNS:
North Africa, Italy

DECORATIONS:
1939-1945 Star, Africa Star, Italy Star, Newfoundland Volunteer Service Medal, Defence Medal, Victory Medal

REGIMENT:
166th (Newfoundland) Field Regiment R.A.

SERIAL #: 971114

Jack March was born on October 8, 1915, the son of Howard and Julia March, and grew up on Bannerman Street in St. John's.

March passed away on July 15, 1969. □□

The information about Jack March comes from an interview with his son Gary March, October 2003.

Left to Right: Jack March, unknown, unknown.
The photo was probably taken in Africa or Italy.

JOHN PETER FINN

DATE ENTERED SERVICE:
June 7,1940

CAMPAIGNS:
D-Day landing, Northwest Europe

DECORATIONS:
Service Star 1939-1945, France and Germany Star, Victory Medal, Newfoundland Volunteer Service Medal 1939-1945, Defence Medal, Dutch Medal of Remembrance

REGIMENT:
59th (Newfoundland) Heavy Regiment R.A., British 6th Airborne

SERIAL #: 970850

I was born on November 10, 1920, in St. John's to Mike and Catherine Finn. I went to school at St. Bon's and played senior hockey with the blue and gold. In addition to hockey, I played senior baseball, soccer, and basketball.

When the war broke out, I joined because everyone else was joining, not because I was patriotic. I went overseas on June 14, 1940, as part of the 4th Contingent. My rank was gunner. Once we arrived in England, we all did various courses in gunnery, driving, and signals. I did a signal course in a place called Harrogate, Yorkshire, that lasted two months. I also did a course to be a driver operator. Then we all came back to the same area and we split up into batteries.

I was in 22nd Battery and stationed in Kent for the most part. We were part of the home defence and we put England in sandbags. They had very little over there. We never had any guns so we were going around with pick handles on our backs so it would look like a gun. Eventually the States started sending over guns, trucks, planes, and boats. Only for them, we would have been lost.

My brother Jim was a pilot in the RAF and was part of the 125 Newfoundland Squadron that flew Mosquitos. He was shot down over the English Channel on January 15, 1943, and was never found. [See story, page 107.]

In March 1944, I was sent to train with the 6th Airborne in Larkhill on the Salisbury Plain, along with nine other members of my regiment. They called up, looking for a Forward Observation Operator, someone who could drive a jeep and operate a wireless. When I arrived, they put me with a bunch of signallers. In addition to the FOO course, we did commando training, conditioning, and five parachute jumps. Once the month of March passed, we could not move out of this area because of security reasons. As the invasion was getting nearer, we did not have time to complete our training.

About a week or so before the invasion, I saw a posting on the wall, and I could see that all the members of my regiment were returning, with the exception of me. I said, "What about me, I came up with that crowd?" "No, you're staying with us," he said, "we need you." That was the only conversation that took place.*

On June 6, we got the word we were going, and I was going in by glider. There were eight in my glider that had a large cargo section for my jeep, while some other Horsas carried 30 infantry. When the plane took off, we could not hear a word, and as we got closer to the coast we received some flak from the enemy. When we were released from the tow rope at the coast, it was just silence. You could hear a pin drop.

We were lucky because we had a good landing. We landed in an orchard near the town of Ranville about nine miles in from the coast. In our landing area there were already five or six gliders on the ground. Others were not as lucky. We passed one that was on fire on the ground. Once we landed, we took the tail off the Horsa and backed the jeep out, and took other supplies. We looked for the regimental sergeant major and he told us that we had to secure positions until daylight. Once we were there for a while we met four or five French civilians in the orchard, Free French Interiors, FFI's. They said, "We'll take you now where you want to go." They took some chances. They let us know where the Germans were and where the best place would be for an observation post, which was a church steeple.

As we came in by gliders we took them by surprise because there was no noise in the glider. They got some surprise coming back from nightclubs. There was a lot of noise and confusion, people speaking German, and people shooting all around. I was a signalman and we did not go into the heavy stuff. These fellas were experienced, and their objective was to save a bridge that they thought the Germans were going to blow. Their mission was a success.

My job as a signalman was to relay firing instructions from battle commanders to artillery operators in the field. When daylight came, we were already set up in the church. The only one we contacted was a British battleship out in the channel [English Channel]. We gave them range and location of German tanks and troops so they could fire on them. That was our first bit of action.

While with the airborne, we stayed around Ranville for a couple of weeks until we got a foothold. We were then in several places in France. I remember one time we were up in this water tower and this sniper came in. He looked down and saw some Germans and said he was going to shoot at one of them. The officer said, "If you shoot from here, it will give away our position, and we'll all be killed." He was turned out to look for another location.

I wanted to go back to my own regiment because I was with a bunch of strangers. If I was going to be killed, I wanted to be with people whom I knew. I had a job to get out of that airborne. They were soon going over the Rhine. I wrote to Captain Lewis Brookes, who worked in the commissioner's office on Victoria Street in London. He was the one who assisted in helping me out.

I was with the 6th Airborne Division until the second week of August when I returned to England for a month's leave. In September I met up with my regiment in Holland. Around this time the Ardennes was happening. We were there one day, and the next thing, the 6th Airborne Division passed by to assist. They were called back from England. I knew four or five of them. I remember them saying, "We're all right now that you're here, you lucky bastard."

The guys in my regiment did not know where I had been during my absence. They were making a big deal about it but I just wanted to keep it low key.

On VE-Day we were in Hamburg, Germany, waiting to get on a train and then a boat to go back to England. We were the army of occupation and things were winding down.

I came home in August 1945. It was a wide awakening. There were no responsibilities and it took a couple of years to come around. At first I worked with the navy, sending back navy boats from St. John's. I also worked as a car salesman and at CJON radio station.

John Finn passed away on October 22, 2004. □□

* The story of how John Finn ended up with the 6th Airborne for the D-Day invasion conflicts with what is in Herb Wells' book *Comrades In Arms*, Volume 1, and G.W.L. Nicholson's book, *More Fighting Newfoundlanders.*

John Finn's photo comes from Herb Wells, *Comrades In Arms*, Volume 1, page 39.

ARTHUR GARRETT DEWLING

DATE ENTERED SERVICE: April 1, 1940

CAMPAIGNS: Northwest Europe

DECORATIONS:
Service Star 1939-1945, France and Germany Star, Victory Medal, Newfoundland Volunteer Service Medal, Defence Medal

REGIMENT:
59th (Newfoundland) Heavy Regiment R.A.

DRAFT: 1st

SERIAL #: 970301

Art Dewling was born in the east end of St. John's on June 5, 1917. He was one of two children born to Joseph and Emily Dewling. He went to school at Bishop Feild and worked at the Newfoundland Savings Bank before the war started. At the age of 22 he enlisted in the artillery and was part of the First Four Hundred. In 1942 Dewling, along with seven others, was wearing the lonely pip of a second lieutenant. On July 17, 1944, the gun area of the 59th was bombed by the Germans in the vicinity of Norrey-en-Bessin. Fortunately nobody was killed in the attack, but there were twelve people injured. Art Dewling was one of these twelve as he was injured in the leg.

"Dewling was a really popular officer and a nice guy," said John Finn of St. John's. "Some were lousy officers, but he was good. He was reasonable. If a fella was ten minutes late, he did not book him. When he got his commission, it did not go to his head. He was also the coach of our football team and we played against the other batteries."

On Dec. 2, 1945, he received his discharge.

Art Dewling died on January 17, 1972. □□

The information about Art Dewling comes from G.W.L. Nicholson, *More Fighting Newfoundlanders*, page 121 and page 262, and from interviews with his son Doug Dewling, October 2003, and with John Finn of St. John's, May 18, 2003.

CHAPTER 6

MERCHANT NAVY

The importance of the Merchant Navy cannot be overestimated. They carried everything the Allies required to feed the war machine. They carried troops, fuel, guns and ammunition, tanks and vehicles of every kind, as well as food and other raw materials. Apart from the normal dangers of the sea, those in the Merchant Navy had to contend with surface raiders, German U-boats, and aircraft attacks. Those who served in the Merchant Navy were part of the longest continuing battle of the war, The Battle of the Atlantic.

THOMAS H. GOODYEAR

CAMPAIGNS:
Battle of the Atlantic

DECORATIONS:
Newfoundland Volunteer Service Medal, Victory Medal, Africa Star, Atlantic Star, Mediterranean Star, 1939-1945 Star, Norway Medal

SHIPS:
Queen of Bermuda, Northern Prince, RMS *Nova Scotia, Fort Amherst, Britanic, Baltrover*

I was born on March 17, 1920, on Welsh's Square overlooking the harbour of St. John's, to Valentine and Elsie Goodyear. My father was a Royal Navy Reservist in World War I. I had some education in the capital city but I went to sea early at the age of sixteen. In the summertime I sailed on various schooners and after three years of this, my mind was made up I was going to sea.

In 1939 I joined the *Queen of Bermuda* where I eventually became a quartermaster. On August 28, 1939, we came in from Havana and received orders to pay off the crew, sign on a skeleton crew and take the ship back to England. She was to be taken into the Royal Navy, which was in their plans when she was built. She was big, fast, and strengthened in many ways, particularly to carry guns. On September 1, we left New York for Belfast, Ireland. Two days later, when the war started, we were mid-Atlantic bound for Belfast. Upon arrival, we had two options. We could remain with the ship to familiarize the new sailors with the working of the ship or to go home. I chose to leave as I had been away for over a year, and I thought it was time to see my parents again. I left Liverpool on one of the Furness Withy passenger ships in a convoy, and on the second day out, one of our ships was torpedoed. This was the first ship that was torpedoed in convoy during the war. Eventually we arrived in St. John's, where I checked into Bishop Feild College to get some tutoring.

In early December, I received a phone call from Furness Withy to inform me that one of their ships, the *Northern Prince*, was in New York and fully loaded with munitions. The deck crew had moved off because they did not want to go to England. As a result, I rounded up the necessary crew and we left St. John's in December aboard the *Fort Amherst* to pick up the *Northern Prince*. Once we arrived in New York, we sailed immediately for England. When we arrived, we were in London about a month. During this time we were discharging cargo, but we could not work at night because of the bombing and the blackout. We also had two guns installed on the *Northern Prince*, one a 4.7 anti-submarine gun and the other was a 3-inch anti-aircraft gun. We were given a gunnery course, and when we sailed, they put on board two naval gunners to help those of us who were selected to operate the guns.

Each time we went back and forth from New York to the UK there would be modifications done on the ship to help fight against various types of mines and later dive-bombers.

The next time we were in the English Channel, the evacuation of Dunkirk was taking place. There was a lot of activity there as you could see the smoke where they were firing at the ships in the channel. We were not involved in the evacuation. We were supposed to take our six lifeboats to Dunkirk, but when we got to Southend they took us off and sent us to the ship. This was done in case the Germans attacked England, we would be there to get the ships out. This did not happen and eventually our lifeboats came back. Then we made our way down the channel and went into Southampton for one purpose. We took on board 30 tons of gold bullion to purchase munitions from the United States.

On the last trip out of London following Dunkirk, we took on some Newfoundlanders and some English sailors, two in particular who were most unusual fellas. They were well educated, well spoken, not very good sailors, but good shipmates and top-notch fellas. They turned out to be communists. I did not find this out until thirty years after the war ended.

We traded back and forth all that summer of 1940, and we ran alone. There were no convoys and we did 20 knots. It was a high-speed ship with two massive diesels. On November 5, 1940, I was in the crow's nest and I wasn't there long before I spotted something on the starboard bow. I reported this to the bridge because it was unusual in those days to see anything, as she was routed in such a fashion to avoid the major shipping lanes. I reported that it looked like a battleship. The next thing, a knock came on the bottom of the crow's nest door and in came the Fourth Officer with a pair of binoculars and an identification book. He peered through the binoculars for a while and he said, "Christ, it's one of the German pocket battleships." He phoned down immediately, gave a 90-degree turn to port, and the engines that were already at full got some more speed somewhere. They sighted us but did not do anything for two reasons. First of all they could have recognized us as one of boats that [German Admiral] Doenitz said not to touch, or they did not want to disclose their own presence. They were after the *Jervis Bay* and her convoy.

About five or six days later, we arrived in Liverpool, and our two unusual fellas disappeared. Nobody knew what happened to them, because they left their clothes, they just went. Thirty years later there was a book written, *A Man Called Intrepid.* As I read through the book, I read at a point where a man had been taken off a British ship, George Thomas Armstrong. Good God, that was one of the communists. The other fella who was with him was Douglas Fraser, a New Zealander. As I read on, it said that Armstrong was hanged in prison for espionage. He was spying for the Germans.

Directly after, I found out why we had such a good summer. When these two communists came with us in the spring of 1940, word went out from Admiral Doenitz to his U-boats, "Do not touch the *Northern Prince*," because these two men were aboard. Now the *Northern, Southern, Eastern,* and *Western* were identical ships with the same profile. Within two months of Scotland Yard taking these two fellas off, the *Northern* was sunk in the Mediterranean with bombs. They torpedoed the *Western* to the west of Ireland, and shortly after, they got the *Southern.*

When these two unusual sailors disappeared, we were tied up alongside the *Nova Scotia*, which was one of Furness Withy's ships that used to run to Newfoundland. I said to myself, "This is a great chance for me to get home," and I signed on. In particular I wanted to get out to see Jessie Windsor, a girl whom I had met when I was ashore in Newfoundland.

It was decided that they were going to make a troop ship out of the *Nova Scotia.* Around February 1941 we left with a large convoy going out to the Mediterranean, but we could not get through because the Germans had control of it. Italy was now in the war and Germany had invaded Greece, and because of this, we had to go around the Cape. When we got north of the equator, or in that area, we were attacked by a submarine or a pack of submarines. There was great excitement. The destroyers were going like hell and sending up starshells. They were shells that go up on a parachute and slope down very slowly. I do not know what the result was, but we just carried on.

In November 1942 we brought troops up to Egypt, landed them, and went through the canal [Suez Canal] at high speed and anchored in Alexandria. While we were anchored here, the battle of El Alamein was at its height. This is where Montgomery decided to make his stand. If Rommel had succeeded in breaking through at El Alamein, our purpose was to stay in Alexandria until the Germans came through. The engineers were to bomb the bridges and we were to take the engineers, but this did not happen, as Montgomery's Eighth Army held.

We then went to Massawa in Ethiopia and took on board 700-900 Italian prisoners, civilians, and several hundred British troops. The day before we arrived in Durban, which is on the southeast coast of Africa, we were torpedoed by a German U-boat. The ship sank within six minutes. It turned out to be, if not the greatest tragedy of the war, pretty close to it. One thousand lives were lost. The ship went down very quickly and everybody was thrown into the water. In addition, there were no lifeboats that got away. We had great difficulty getting near the rafts as the Italians used to drive us away, and there were more of them than us. We finished up with hand-to-hand fighting with the Italians. When you are faced with certain things, there are things that you would do that you would not dream of otherwise.

In addition to the bitter fighting, there were sharks that took a lot of the people. "Hundreds of those in the water disappeared within a few minutes. Some fought on until overcome by exhaustion; others were choked by the slimy oil."* Of the 114 of *Nova Scotia*'s crew, only 14 survived.* Somehow I survived this carnage after being in the water for 40 hours.

We were sunk by U-177, whose captain was a Robert Gysae. When he realized that he had sunk a ship with his allies on board, he swore his crew to secrecy. As a matter of fact I have a copy of his logbook.

This second version of the story about being torpedoed by a German U-boat off the southeast coast of Africa was recorded by Veterans Affairs Canada in a project called "Heroes Remember." It is used here with permission.

> *We loaded prisoners in Abyssinia, Italians, with no escort, and we set sail for Durban. It was a clear morning, scattered rain showers, and our ship took two torpedoes. Our ship sank in less than five minutes. Now at that time all the prisoners were on deck*

and had just eaten breakfast. The ship rolled over down to the head and sank before we had a chance to fire. We found ourselves in the water. I knew there were sharks around there, and the water was covered with bunker oil, which was like tar, black and thick. I said to my buddy, "I'm going to cover myself with tar, and I suggest that you do the same." He did. There were no sharks around at the time, but I was hoping it would discourage them a bit. That was 9 am, and by dark, we were still in the water. If you went near a raft, the Italian prisoners would drive you away, because they had charge of the rafts. They knew us because we had different life-jackets.

We suffered out that night and stayed awake in some fashion. By now there were sharks around, and they were taking people. By dark that night, I said to my buddy Hill, "If we don't get in one of those rafts, you'll never see another daylight." He said, "Let's take one." The thinking process was slow by then, and I did not know quite what he meant. He said, "There is a big raft there with 13 people on it. Let's take it." We go up alongside it and pull a man off and hold him under. I kind of shook my head. He said, "You look after me and I will do it. If anyone comes near me, you nail them." This was more or less the agreement. Before long, they were gone, and we had the raft. There was one fella left on board, and he had one arm. Hill left him alone. We spent a second night in the water. Sometime during the night a Portuguese Man of War, called the Alfonso *something or other, came and took us aboard.*

I finally found my way home and was set for a Second Mate's ticket, which I got, and within a month Jess and I were married. Once I got my ticket, I rejoined the Furness Withy Company again as a junior navigating officer on the *Fort Amherst.* I remained with that company until the war was over and beyond. The day before VE-Day, sometime in May, we went through the Cape Cod Canal and were approaching Point Judith. Coming in the opposite direction was another vessel, and we were going to pass close by, she on one side and us on the other. As I was on watch at the time, I could see the periscope of a submarine, but the man coming to relieve me could not see anything. He just let it go. We met the American boat at the buoy, and within twenty minutes, she was nailed. It was a periscope I had seen, and for reasons I don't know, the other fella got it and we didn't.

Further to that, as a result of another strange set of circumstances, I happened to be the pilot on the first German cruiser that came to Canada after the war. As luck would have it, the captain on board was a friend of Robert Gysae, who was by now Admiral Gysae. I told the captain that he had sunk the ship I was on. As a result of this chance conversation, when Christmas rolled around, I received a Christmas card from Admiral Gysae. For the next ten years or so we would exchange Christmas cards. Eventually he invited my wife and me to visit him at his summer home in the Black Forest. While I was in England, I went to see two other friends of mine who were on the *Nova Scotia.* They were horrified that I was even considering going to visit Robert Gysae. Their disapproval made me feel very uneasy about the fact. As a result of that, I never did go to meet Admiral Gysae, and I have been kicking myself ever since. He is now dead. An acquaintance of mine whose mother tongue is German made some inquiries about Robert Gysae. He survived the war, which was unusual in itself, as those who served in the U-boats got an awful pasting. He became an admiral and was attached to the German Embassy in Washington for three years. His wife is still alive in Germany, so it would be nice to speak to her.

Tom Goodyear lives in St. John's with his wife Jessie Windsor Goodyear, who is also a veteran. Her story appears on page 74. □□

* Ratcliff, J.D. "Death off Durban," *The Reader's Digest,* Volume 87, August 1965, pages 34-39.

JAMES ANTHONY HAYDEN

DATE ENTERED SERVICE:
Merchant Navy 1938
U.S. Navy 1943

CAMPAIGNS:
Battle of the Atlantic, Battle of the Pacific

SHIPS:
Fort Amherst, Fort Townsend, Nerissa, Western Prince, Ville D'anvers, Havorn, Virginia, SS *Indra,* LV *Stanford,* USS *Zebra*

I was born on November 11, 1911, in Petite Forte to Patrick and Winifred Hayden. For a small community, Petite Forte had a lot of men in the armed forces during the Second World War. In my family there were four of us who did their duty. I was in the Merchant Navy and the US Navy. My brother Gordon was in the Royal Navy and was involved in the evacuation of Dunkirk. In a rowboat, he rowed into the beach to pick up Allied soldiers and then rowed back. I had a brother Patrick who was also in the Merchant Navy and was torpedoed off the coast of Scotland. My older brother Legouri, who was known as Gory, served in the Newfoundland Overseas Forestry Unit for six years.

I have been on the sea all my life. I went to the Labrador with my brother fishing, where I stayed for two years in Port Hope Simpson. When I came back, I went out on the Grand Banks on one of Crosbie's draggers. In October 1937 we took over the *Prospero*, which was an old government ship that was sold to the Greeks. We got waterlogged off the coast of Ireland in a storm, but we survived even though she was on her side.

In 1938 I joined the Merchant Navy. The day before England declared war on Germany in 1939, we left New York aboard the *Fort Amherst* with stops at Halifax and St. John's. Another ship that I served on was the *Western Prince*. This was a much larger ship owned by Furness Withy. I joined her in New York with a whole bunch of Newfoundlanders, and we went to Vancouver to load up supplies for England. We came back through Panama. On Christmas Eve 1939 we had a German ship behind us with a British flag flying over the swastika. Her name was the *Dusseldorf* and she had been captured by the British. They took her to Jamaica and that is where they interned them. We went there as well because we had broken our propellers.

While on the *Western Prince* in the Strait of Dover, we were attacked by a German plane that did a lot of damage. The plane was a Junker and I was the only fella on deck because we were on night watch. I heard this plane coming, and at first I thought it might have been a friendly plane as they were bombing Dover terrible. He had laid a lot of magnetic mines, and on his way home, he found us and used his machine gun. As he came closer to our ship, he attacked us with 1800 bullets a minute. Our ship looked like a troop ship. He made three attacks. He was so close, I think I could have hit the plane. He was a real daredevil. I happened to be standing on one of the ladders of the ship, and he hit the handrail where I was. Bullets went down between my feet, over my head, and behind me. They were 20-mm and they could have ripped me apart but they never hit me. Then I ran by the ship's swimming pool and I stopped next to a stanchion or a post. He must have put 50 bullets in it. The heavy paint came off on my sweater but I still was not hit. Finally, we manned the guns, but when I arrived there, the gunner was nowhere to be seen. As a result of his attacks, we had to go back to London. There was nothing too severe but our radio shack was all shot up, along with the lifeboats and the rigging.

In February 1943 I was a quartermaster aboard the *Fort Amherst* in port in St. John's. There were some ships in the harbour that needed men so I joined an American oil tanker along with a fella Conners from St. John's. We picked up a convoy on the Grand Banks and by the second night the convoy was attacked by U-boats. We had 57 ships in the convoy and half way over they told us to split up and go on our own. That was the thing to do but it was very dangerous. They told us we had lost 21 ships, but I have no proof of that. I do know we lost ships because I saw them get hit.

While in New York, I had registered for the draft with a fella from Harbour Buffet. We were not supposed to do this but we did it anyway. I put my name in for the draft because I wanted to get my citizen papers. When I got back, I had received a letter that I was inducted into the US Army. I was only in the army for about three hours as we went to a building in New York where there were about 3000 men. They were asking people who wanted to join the Marines, and when they asked about the navy, I put up my hand. I was then in the navy but then I had a problem. I told a naval officer that I was an alien. He told me not to worry as I was in the navy now. We did our training in Samson, New York, which was near the Canadian border, and then I got shipped to San Francisco. As a result of my experience at sea, I became a petty officer at boot camp. In San Francisco, before I went to the Pacific, I asked to see the captain of the base and I told him my problem. I was eventually sworn in as an American citizen.

In July 1943 we were on our way to the Pacific in a troop ship and I remember being on watch up in the crow's nest. I spotted land on our starboard bow, which later turned out to be Guam. That night an officer came to me and told me that when I had reported land it was 34 miles away and that the radar had not even picked it up. Radar was relatively new but he told me that I had really good eyesight. From there we went ashore in a place called Espirtu Santu, which was a Portuguese colony island. The navy had a base there.

Next I joined a ship to lay torpedo nets. She was a Liberty ship, which had a big deck space and big cargo holes. She had plenty of guns on her, but she was not a fighting ship. We were a work ship. We had to load the nets in Pearl Harbor and go with the fleet. We put in the torpedo nets where there were no harbours. There would be a lot of ships anchored. These were not fighting ships, but cargo ships. They were filled with everything from guns, ammunition, tanks, food and other vital supplies. We would put these very heavy torpedo nets around these boats. I had gone to net training school and I was in charge of putting those nets together.

The last net that we put out was in Iwo Jima, where there was some fierce fighting. From there we went back to San Francisco as our ship had been smashed up. While there, the war ended and I was discharged. I wanted to stay in the navy but I had gotten married to a woman from St. Bernard's, Newfoundland. After the war all the shipyards were closing up and there were no jobs available. We stayed in the United States and made our home there.

Jim Hayden lives in Brooklyn, New York. □□

WALLACE DICKS

DATE ENTERED SERVICE:
1940

CAMPAIGNS:
Battle of the Atlantic

SCHOONERS: *Bal D'or*

I was born on August 5, 1919, in Harbour Buffet to Gerald and Jessie Dicks. Prior to the war, I was fishing on the Grand Banks. With the outbreak of the war, I, along with many others from my community, volunteered for the navy. For some unknown reason I was not accepted. After fishing on the Grand Banks, I went to the dockyard in Pictou, Nova Scotia, where I joined the schooner *Bal D'or*. This boat was one that the Warehams took from the French on the Grand Banks during the war. From Pictou, we went on to Halifax to pick up a load of lumber and took it to Egypt. This was my first trip as a merchant seaman. On our return trip, while on our way to the base in St. John's, we hit a really bad day. As a result of this stormy weather, we were shipwrecked up around Trepassy. We were there for a day as we got our gear off. From St. John's we returned to Halifax to pick up some more lumber for another trip to Egypt. We delivered our lumber and then we had to wait to get a charter to Newfoundland. A charter meant we were waiting for something to bring back. We were in Cyprus for about a month. From there we went to Spain to pick up a load of salt and head for the Labrador.

I was in England a number of times, but I do remember one time there, and I sold all my clothes, which only came to about $10.00. From there, whatever was to be done, you would get a job and do it.

My job on the schooner was cook. I had no training for this, and I just became a cook. We had a crew of 12 that were all from Newfoundland. On the schooner, conditions were rough, and there was very little to eat. We did not get any leave while I served with the Merchant Navy. If we were in port for a period of time, all we did was work, like painting and the general upkeep of the boat.

I was involved in convoy duty once. The convoy had between twenty and thirty vessels that went from Halifax to Egypt. With this exception, we sailed alone. The schooners that I sailed on had no weapons. Fortunately, we did not have any encounters with U-boats or surface raiders. I do remember the British corvettes would come by on the Grand Banks. The person in charge would blow their whistle once, twice, or three times. Then everybody would go out in the dory and stay behind the vessel until it was clear again.

I stayed with Warehams' the entire war and I would do it all over again.

Wallace Dicks passed away on November 18, 2004. □□

JOSEPH LEO PRIM

DATE ENTERED SERVICE:
1943

CAMPAIGNS:
Battle of the Atlantic

DECORATIONS:
Atlantic Star, British Merchant Navy Medal, Newfoundland Volunteer Service Medal, Victory Medal

SHIPS:
Fort Townshend, Fort Amherst

I was born on Shaw's Lane in St. John's on January 13, 1927, to Matthew and Theresa Prim. I went to school at Holy Cross, and before I joined the Merchant Navy, I worked at some gas stations. At the age of sixteen I joined the Merchant Navy as I was too young to sign up anywhere else. In addition to this, my father had gone to sea at the age of thirteen. He was a student at St. Bon's when he ran away from school and stowed away on one of Crosbie's vessels. On their way back from South America they were captured by a German raider. His ship was sunk, and my father and the rest of the crew became prisoners of war. They spent the remainder of the First World War in Germany.

In order to join the Merchant Navy you had to go to the shipping office in St. John's and sign six-month articles. At that time the shipping office was located down across from the war memorial [Duckworth Street], on back of O'Leary's. Once your six months were up, you could renew your article or sign on with another ship. In those days, on merchant ships, there were a lot of young people. There were a few older hands, but very few. Usually, when young people were taken aboard, they were assigned to the galley, in the catering department. When I boarded the ship, I went on as an Ordinary Seaman which was up on the deck. My duties were to help out the Able Seamen and take orders from the bosun who was in charge on deck. At this time these vessels were run strictly by British standards, and the class distinction was adhered to at all times. The officers very rarely spoke to the crew unless they were giving orders or the crew were in trouble, as strict discipline was maintained.

We did a lot of convoy work. We would go out over the Grand Banks or somewhere in the mid-Atlantic to pick up a convoy. As an ordinary seaman I knew nothing about charts or navigation. We would go into Halifax, Boston, and sometimes Sydney. Other times we might leave New York with a convoy and go to Halifax, and leave again with another convoy. As we were part of the British Furness Withy Fleet, we served as the commodore ship. This meant that the commodore traveled on the ship or the captain of the ship was the commodore, and he was in charge of the convoy.

Traveling in convoys was scary around Newfoundland in foggy weather as there was no radar. In restricted visibility most of the time, you did not know where you were. If you were in a convoy with thirty or forty ships in black thick fog, especially in nighttime, it was scary business.

There were a lot of ships sunk, many outside the Narrows in St. John's. Sometimes there were enemy subs around as the navy would be dropping depth charges. You could be on alert or standby for hours. On board our ship we had a 3.3, a cannon, along with a machine gun. There was a gunnery school on the South Side [St. John's] and this is where I did training. When we came into port and you were single, you had to go to the gunnery school. We trained anywhere from a day to a couple of weeks.

I remember being part of the biggest convoy that ever went across. There were 130 ships in it and we were up to the front of the convoy. About 6:00 am we spotted a target coming in from the east. We were out on the Grand Banks and we did not know what it was. We were afraid it was a German raider, and as a result, we formed up stations. Instead of the enemy, it was the *Queen Mary.* It was a beautiful morning and the ocean was just as flat as this table. She was coming down full speed at 35 knots. When she passed through the centre of the convoy, all her crews were on the guns. As she passed each ship, she dipped her flag to them. That stands out in my memory.

From the time I joined the Merchant Navy I served for two years continuously. When you arrived in port, the crew on board made sure that we would get out for a few beer. In addition, we were permitted to have a half dozen beer a day, and the officers were entitled to a bottle of liquor a week. The price was 10 cents for a can of beer, and 10 cents for a package of cigarettes.

When the war ended, I had just turned eighteen. The Merchant Navy played a vital role. The Americans say that the war would not have been won without logistics, and I can see that now, how true that statement was. The Merchant Navy carried everything from troops, fuel, artillery, and anything else needed for the war. Whatever went overseas, Merchant Navy carried it.

Joe Prim lives in St. John's. □□

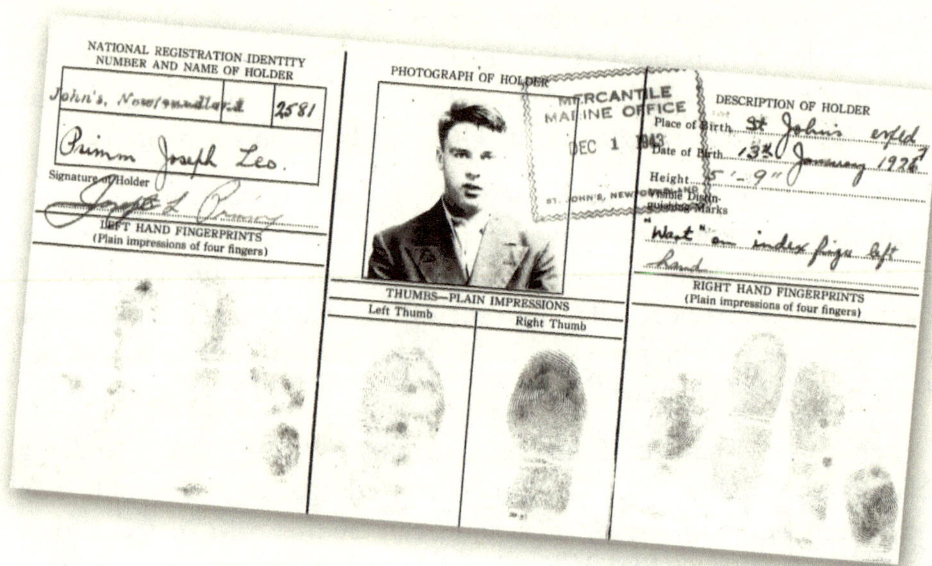

NATIONAL REGISTRATION IDENTITY NUMBER AND NAME OF HOLDER

John's, Newfoundland | 2581

Primm Joseph Leo.

Signature of Holder

Joseph L Prim

LEFT HAND FINGERPRINTS
(Plain impressions of four fingers)

PHOTOGRAPH OF HOLDER

MERCANTILE MARINE OFFICE
DEC 1 1943
ST. JOHN'S, NEWFOUNDLAND

THUMBS—PLAIN IMPRESSIONS

Left Thumb | Right Thumb

DESCRIPTION OF HOLDER

Place of Birth St Johns Nfld

Date of Birth 13th January 1926

Height 5'-9"

Visible Distinguishing Marks "Wart" on index finger left hand

RIGHT HAND FINGERPRINTS
(Plain impressions of four fingers)

Joe Prim's Merchant Navy ID card.

ARTHUR EDWARD WHITE

DATE ENTERED SERVICE:
March 7,1940

CAMPAIGNS:
Battle of the Atlantic

DECORATIONS:
Victory Medal, Volunteer Service Medal 1939-1945, and three bars

SHIPS: *Curlew*

I was born on July 30, 1919, in Torbay to Henry and Emmie White. Before the war broke out, I was fishing in Torbay with my father and brother. Soon after, I went to St. John's to volunteer for the navy. At the same time there was a boat in the harbour full of TNT. The navy needed this to be delivered to England as she was in a dire need of this precious cargo. As a result of my sea experience, the navy indicated that they would like me to be part of a crew to bring this trawler to England. In order to be a part of this crew, I joined the Merchant Marine in St. John's.

In July 1940, with a crew of 12, we left St. John's. There were six of us from Newfoundland, of which three were from Torbay. Eli Codner and Stan White were the other two. On our passage over in the *Curlew* we did not have any problems with U-boats, but once we reached the channel [English Channel] we encountered some aerial attacks from the Luftwaffe. On July 20, we landed at Fallmouth and the navy took immediate control over her. Our cargo was like gold dust to them.

Being part of the Merchant Marine, we were at everything. We were delivering things here and there. We could be gone all day and return at night. Other times we could be gone two or three days. Sometimes, we could be involved in taking ships off the rocks that were beached. They were beached because they might have received a shot in the bow from the enemy. Our job was to try and get them off, which involved a lot of small boat work. If we were successful in getting a ship off the rocks, we would bring her into Portsmouth. They would have that ship repaired in no time, and she would be back on the sea again.

After we were discharged from a ship, we had the option of going to another one. Even though I was in a shipping pool, they could not take my choice away from me. However, because of my sea experience, I had difficulty in avoiding the shipping pool. Once you signed up for delivering TNT there was no getting away from it. Delivering this cargo was a dangerous job. If we got hit at all, it would have been disastrous. Sometimes when we were not as busy, we were sent into the pools to train the navy recruits in small boat training. In a small boat I could take a paddle and do anything.

I was on so many boats during the war. I cannot remember their names. What I do remember were the poor living conditions aboard the boat. Food was scarce. When you go up on deck and you can smell food from other ships, you are hungry. I remember taking a cake of hard bread and dipping it in tea or water. There was not much to eat but plenty to drink. If someone else did not drink his share, you could probably get his share also.

Our shifts were four hours in duration, four on and four off, which was one of the dirtiest watches you could ever be involved in.

In 1944, Eli Codner and I came home. I remember we were up in the Newfoundland Hotel drinking beer and these two or three Yanks came in from Pepperrell. We were there with our tams and navy coats on so they knew we were on our water. We told them we were just after receiving our money and we were not going at it anymore, as the war was nearing an end. One of these Yanks was a master sergeant, and he asked us to come down and see him to see if he could get us a job. We went down and the next thing I knew I was driving a cement mixer.

Looking back on it all now, I supposed I was scared, and I was not an easy fella to scare when I was young. I remember a lot of my good buddies went to the bottom too. Now today, I am a member of Branch 10 of the Royal Canadian Legion. Over the years most of my discharge papers from the pools have been lost or misplaced. There are plenty of people in my situation as we did not feel that these papers were important.

Art White lives in Torbay. □□

A recent photo of Art White.

NEWFOUNDLAND
1939
1945
FORESTRY UNIT

CHAPTER 7

□□

Newfoundland Forestry Unit

In November 1939 there was a need to recruit a civilian workforce to do logging in Great Britain. Initially, those who signed up agreed to serve for a six-month period from the date they landed in the British Isles. They then had the option of returning home, signing on again, or transferring to another branch of the armed forces. Their salary was $2.00 a day or $12.00 a week. Of this total, it was agreed that $1.00 per working day would be sent back to Newfoundland. These loggers were a specialized workforce and provided vital timber for pit-props that were used in mining. When many loggers transferred to other branches, the British government tried to convince them not to leave. "They urged the men to remain in their job and emphasized that they would be providing a greater service to the war effort than if they joined the armed forces."* In further drafts, recruits had to agree to stay on until the end of hostilities.

* Curran, Tom. *They Also Served.*

GEORGE CHARLES PENNEY

DATE ENTERED SERVICE:
July 15, 1941

DECORATIONS:
Defence Medal, Newfoundland Volunteer Service Medal, Forestry Medal

SERIAL #: 3542

I was born on on August 21, 1919, in St. John's to Sam Robert and Irene Penney. I was reared on Quidi Vidi Road, but we also lived in Rabbittown for a few years. By 1932, the year of the riot at the Colonial Building, we moved to Oxen Pond Road. I attended school on Middle Battery Road, followed by Bond Street school.

Between1939 and 1941 I was working for the government at the Colonial Building. When the war broke out, most of my friends had already enlisted in the navy, army, or air force. As a result I joined the navy when they first started recruiting but I was not accepted. I received a badge that stated, "For King and Country I have volunteered." My badge # was 129.

By the time I joined the forestry, I was working at Fort Pepperrell as a truck driver making $4.50 a day. That was good money then. The recruiting office for the unit was located in the Colonial Building. At the time I joined, there were not a lot left from St. John's, but volunteers were picked up all across the island. When I joined, we had to sign for the duration of the war, unlike earlier drafts that had the option to leave after six months. I also had a younger brother who joined the forestry.

We left St. John's by train and went to Port aux Basques. Next we boarded the *Caribou* and sailed to Sydney. We were in Halifax about a week. Finally we left on a Norwegian whaler and had a 21-day voyage, landing in Liverpool. From there we went to the north of Scotland.

I drove trucks all over Scotland. I delivered logs to the mill, transported the carpenters around. For the most part, I dealt with the construction crowd. We would work every day, except Sunday, and on Saturday half a day. Our pay was $2.50 a day, but we only received half of this as the remainder was sent home.

While in Scotland I also volunteered for the Home Guard. It was much like the Home Guard here. We had guard duty and drill every Sunday morning. When I was granted leave I generally went to Edinburgh, but I liked Aberdeen and Dundee also.

When the war ended I had no regrets. I arrived home on September 11, 1945.

George Penney lives in St. John's. □□

JOHN JOSEPH QUIGLEY

DATE ENTERED SERVICE: Unknown

CAMPAIGNS: Battle of the Atlantic

SHIP: HMS *Hood*

SERIAL #: NFU 0408
PJX212487

Jack Quigley was born on August 29, 1916, to Thomas and Catherine Quigley of Torbay. During the Depression he worked at various logging camps in Corner Brook.

Quigley joined the Newfoundland Forestry Unit along with his brother Raymond. On January 23, 1940, they arrived in Liverpool as part of the 2nd Contingent.

Eventually, Quigley transferred from the forestry unit to the Royal Navy where his rank was Ordinary Seaman. He did his training in Portsmouth. His first ship was the *Hood*, which he represented as a boxer, fighting sailors from other ships. On May 24, 1941, the HMS *Hood* was sunk by the German battleship *Bismarck*. Only three men of the *Hood*'s crew of 1416 survived. "Sixteen Newfoundlanders lost their lives that day of which thirteen had only recently transferred from the Forestry."* □□

* Wells, Herbert, *Under the White Ensign*, Volume 1.

The information about John Quigley comes from an interview with Austin Kinsella, August 25, 1999.

CHAPTER 8

□□

U.S. ARMY & BRITISH ARMY

Newfoundlanders and some who would become Newfoundlanders also volunteered for the U.S. Army and British Army.

THOMAS JOSEPH HOULIHAN

DATE ENTERED SERVICE:
November 21, 1942

CAMPAIGNS:
Sicily, Italy

DECORATIONS:
American Campaign Medal, Good Conduct Medal, Victory Medal, European African Middle Eastern Campaign Medal, Bronze Star, Purple Heart

BATTALION: 10th Engineers BN, 3rd Infantry Division

Joe Houlihan was born in Flatrock, Newfoundland, on October 20, 1920, to Maurice Houlihan and Mary Quigley. He was the oldest son of nine children. After leaving Flatrock, he worked as a butcher's helper on the Furness Red Cross ships which his father served on for fourteen years. He secured legal entry papers admitting him to the United States. He also worked for two years with Fletcher's Shipyards in Hoboken, New Jersey.

According to a letter received by his father, Pte. Houlihan had gone through the campaign in Sicily. He had been attached to the engineers and it is presumed that he moved into Italy with the Fifth Army. On

September 2, 1943, Houlihan was killed in Salerno, Italy. He is buried at the Sicily-Rome American Cemetery and Memorial in Nettuno, Italy. There is a monument in Flatrock today in honour of Houlihan, with the Stars and Stripes flying over it. In addition, Salerno Place in Torbay is named in his honour. □□

The information about Joe Houlihan comes from Gene Quigley, *The Quigleys of Torbay.*

LEONARD WILLIAM DOMMAN

DATE ENTERED SERVICE: 1941

CAMPAIGNS: Northwest Europe

REGIMENT: 3rd Infantry

SERIAL #: 17047605

I was born on June 1, 1917, in St. Paul, Minnesota, to Henry and Elizabeth Domman. When the Japanese made the sneak attack on Pearl Harbor, it put me in great fear. I knew we were not prepared for war at that time. It also made me hate the Japanese military and not the Japanese people. As a result I, like many others, enlisted in the armed forces. I did so because I loved my country and I was willing to die to defend our American way of life. I picked the infantry because it was the only branch of service in our area.

I went to basic training in Fort Snelling, Minnesota. It was extremely hard work. We drilled from morning to sundown. The first day included a 25-mile, full field-pack hike. It was a new way of life, a drastic change of lifestyle for me. All day long the sergeant gave orders, and our job was to obey and not ask questions. The only break was at mealtimes. At the end of the day we were exhausted and just collapsed in our bunks. At times I almost felt like I was in prison. It made a man out of you, that is, if it didn't kill you first. Eventually, after a month or so, I adjusted to this new way of life

We arrived in Newfoundland in June 1942 and were stationed at Fort Pepperrell in St. John's. I was a supply sergeant. During my stay in Newfoundland, I met my wife-to-be, Irene Randell of Port Rexton, Newfoundland, one Sunday afternoon on a bus. I believe it was love at first sight.

By 1943 we left Newfoundland and went back to the States for further training. Eventually, we made our way over to France but it was after D-Day. We saw some action in France, and after that we moved into Germany. We captured a lot of Germans and put them in prison camps. When the war ended I was still in Germany and anxious to return home. We treated our prisoners really well compared to the Japanese. I have friends who were prisoners with the Japanese and they can tell you stories that would make your hair stand on end.

I remember going through the concentration camps. They were unbearable. There were bones piled as high as your house. I saw the ovens where they killed the Jewish people. I also remember seeing [General George] Patton. Another thing that comes to mind. We did not enter Berlin. We let the Russians go first and they took all the glory. That was a mistake. We could have gone in. Eventually, we made our way back to England and we came home on the *Queen Mary.*

When I look back on it all now, I think the Japanese military were cowardly in their attack on Pearl Harbor. I remember hating the Germans during the war, which was interesting because my father was born in Germany. As a matter of fact, because of my background, my mail was always inspected. This made me feel uncomfortable but I understood the reason for this. Before the war, I was training for a job as a tool and die maker. The war came and forced me to change my plans. I never did get to pursue the career that I was interested in. After the war, I moved to California with my war bride. Irene was one of the thousands of women from Newfoundland to marry American servicemen. I ended up working with AT & T telephone company.

Leonard Domman lives in California. □□

PETER THOMAS ROBINSON

DATE ENTERED SERVICE:
May 1943

CAMPAIGNS:
England, Far East

REGIMENT:
47th Anti-Aircraft Division, 24th Advanced Base Workshop, 25th Advanced Base Workshop

I was born on May 15, 1925, in Bridlington, England, to Sidney Steward and Lillian Mary Robinson. When the war broke out in September 1939, I was fourteen years old. As the war went on, we were bombed by the Germans, and at the age of sixteen I became a dispatch driver with the fire service. As a result I was all over the place in the bombing. I lived halfway up the Yorkshire Coast, right opposite Germany, and we got bombed to hell. All they had to do was cross the water and go into the industrial areas. If they hit heavy on the anti-aircraft or the aircraft, which they probably did, they would turn back and drop their bombs on us as they went by. When the German bombers came over, you wanted to jump up into the air and tear them down with your hands. In the fire service we were two days on duty with a day off which was only 12 hours actually. And everybody did fire watch for the bombing. My father was a sergeant in the special police and my mother was an ambulance driver. As a result you did not see much of your family.

I remember looking up and seeing the bombs coming down, and you knew that somebody, perhaps twenty or thirty people, were going to be killed. Sometimes you would even see a plane go down.

At the age of seventeen I volunteered for the army, and I joined as soon as I turned eighteen. Everybody was joining, and we were in the middle of a desperate situation. I was interested in joining the air force but my ears were no good. As a boy I had been in the ATC or Air Training Corps. This was something like the Air Cadets. My basic training was in Markeaton Park in Darbisher and it lasted about three months. We arrived from all over England to Darbisher's Station. We were collected by some sergeants and were taken to where we had our basic training. While here, we had our uniforms just about thrown at us. We were then taken to this big room and given a lecture. The first thing they had, of course, was a rifle. The sergeant then said, "Whatever you do, always make sure that your rifle is unloaded, and never point it at anybody or pull the trigger unless you are in action." And with that, he pointed the rifle and pulled the trigger. There was this almighty bloody bang. The guy at the top of the room gave the big screech and fell down with blood pouring out of him. Our hair just stood up on end. Here it was all a set-up. He had some red dye in his old uniform. We thought he was killed. I never ever forgot that. After I did my basic training, I was first with the 47th Anti-Aircraft Division in England, which was stationed up and down the coast. We fired on the bombers as they came over.

After a while the preparation for the invasion was coming up. I was involved in the technical aspects of the invasion, like waterproofing the tanks. I was in Camp C10, just outside Southampton. I remember seeing the American 101st Airborne and the British Airborne. I was attached to a French Canadian regiment, the Regiment of Chaudiere River, but only temporarily. They got an awful hammering and as a result took heavy casualties. I was also attached to the 89th Anti-Tank

Regiment, the Liverpool Irish. I can still hear the racket now, BOOM, BOOM, BOOM coming from the massive naval armada bombing the coast of France. There is no distance at all between England and France.

After all that was over, instead of going across to France as we expected, we were sent down to the Far East. D-Day was the start of the downfall of Germany, and as things were going pretty well they took the bulk of the armour that was left and sent them down to where the trouble was, down in the Far East with the Japanese. While in the Far East I was with the Fourteenth British Army. Now these numbers mean nothing because one half of the army might be doing one thing and the other half doing another. Then an army was split into divisions, and divisions split into corps, and corps into companies, and companies into platoons.

I was not involved in any actual combat in the Far East. We were in the 24th Advanced Base Workshop, which, if there had to be action, we would have been right up in the line repairing whatever had to be repaired. I was a driver mechanic with the engineers, and I repaired trucks, jeeps, and arms carriers.

Next we went on the invasion of Malaya. I suppose this was the only time you might say that I was injured. We went ashore in a buffalo tank, which was something like a tank but the top was cut off. As a result we were open, but it floated and the tracks would scull them along. During this invasion, the war was technically over but there was some shooting. I did give my arm a severe burn on the exhaust of this thing. We went ashore, stayed there for a while, and then we went back to the ship. We went back to India, joined our regiment at Bangalore, then we drove down as a unit to Madras, which is on the southwest tip of India, got on a ship and went back this time to Singapore. We occupied this, and by this time, the Japanese were getting worn down, the little bastards. I remember one particular place, Changi, which was an airfield. It was also a place where they kept our prisoners. Oh, they tortured them. There were even messages written on the wall in blood.

While in the Far East, I always remember worrying like hell about what was happening at home. I was aware, however, that after D-Day, the Germans had more than enough of their own problems to worry about.

On Christmas Day 1945, our first peacetime Christmas in six years, we were in Singapore. We were on our way to see my friend, Trev Shaw, so we could all go up to get something to eat. We were just about there when we heard this fire engine coming, BANG, BANG, BANG. There was a crowd cheering and here were a bunch of sergeants driving this old fire engine which was civilian red. Somehow or other they got it going. They were all half drunk, and who could blame them? They came past us, ringing the bell and cheering. There must have been between eight and ten of them. When they got up and turned the corner, they rolled over and went into the ditch. We ran up and a lot of them got thrown clear. I dived underneath as it was upside down. I could see that there was somebody there. I tried to drag him out, but he was pinned and could not move. Suddenly, I realized I was wet, saturated. I realized it was gasoline. The tank was upside down, up above me, and the gasoline was all coming down on me.

I turned around to say something to Trev, as he was right behind me, to get the hell out of this. When I turned around, here he was, right behind me with a cigarette lit, hanging out of his face. Well, if my hair ever stood up, that was the day that it did. He must have suddenly realized the situation. Somehow or other he curled his lip back and stuck the cigarette in his mouth and chewed it up, swallowed it, and it lit. The rest is a blur. The crowd had gathered by that time and they dragged us out. They brought me down the road and threw me into a pond to neutralize the gas. I am not sure what happened to Trev. Luckily nobody was killed. The driver was hurt around his legs but it was not too serious.

I did not get back to England until 1947. I never came home to any marching bands, nobody even knew I was home. When I arrived home, the place was wrecked, industry was wrecked. There was food rationing for years. The Americans came home to the G.I. Bill to help them get a start in life. I got nothing, not a thing.

I came to Newfoundland in 1957 for work and experience. I expected to stay for 18 months and, of course, I never got away. I met my wife-to-be, Sue Randell of Port Rexton, on a blind date. Looking back on it now, there were good times and bad, but I made a lot of good friends. It is something to be proud of.

Pete Robinson lives in Mount Pearl. □□

Two members of the 2nd Contigent
Date of Enlistment: December 31, 1939

Mike J. Nolan
JX 180986
Discharged: January 18, 1946

Fred Nolan
JX 180987 O.S.
Killed in action aboard the HMS *Avenger*
November 15, 1942.

Jack Williams
166th [Newfoundland]
Field Regiment R.A.

Joe Power, RAF
Serial #: 1006077

REFERENCES

Curran, Thomas. *They Also Served.* St. John's: Jesperson Publishing, 1987.

Kavanagh, Robert L. *W force: The Canadian Army and the Defence of Newfoundland in the Second World War.* M.A. Thesis, Memorial University of Newfoundland, 1995.

Lake, Harold. *Perhaps They Left Us Up There.* St. John's: Harry Cuff Publications, Ltd., 1995.

Nicholson, G.W.L. *More Fighting Newfoundlanders.* St. John's: Government of Newfoundland and Labrador, 1969.

Quigley, Gene. *The Quigleys of Torbay.* Document archived in the Newfoundland Provincial Archives, 1998.

Ratcliff, J.D. "Death Off Durban." *The Reader's Digest.* Vol. 87, August 1965.

Wells, Herbert. *Comrades In Arms,* Volume 1. St. John's: self-published, 1986.

Wells, Herbert. *Under the White Ensign,* Volume 1. St. John's: self-published, 1977.

GENE P. QUIGLEY was born in St. John's in 1964 and attended St. Patrick's Elementary and Brother Rice High School before earning a B.A. at Memorial University in 1988. He is a Cub Leader with the 1st St. Joseph's Scouting Movement and is also a member of the Bishop Abraham Elementary School Council. He lives with his wife Cindy Randell and their three children in St. John's.

www.ingramcontent.com/pod-product-compliance
Lightning Source LLC
LaVergne TN
LVHW090949080826
845145LV00003B/940

* 9 7 8 1 8 9 4 3 7 7 2 1 8 *